WE INTERRUPT THIS BROADCAST ...

A Veteran Looks Back On His WWII Tour Of Duty

Paul Sikorski

Waldenhouse Publishers, Inc.
Walden, Tennessee

Cover painting by Angela Serre
Editing, type and design by Karen Paul Stone
Published by Waldenhouse Publishers, Inc.
100 Clegg Street, Signal Mountain, Tennessee 37377 USA
Printed in the United States of America
Case binding ISBN: 978-1-935186-93-9
Perfect binding: ISBN 978-1-935186-95-3
Library of Congress Control Number 2017908266
   Autobiographical account of a young man's transition
   from citizen to soldier in the United States Army Signal
   Corps in WWII, his tour of duty in Britain before D-Day
   and in France after, plus two epilogues of the post war
   period related to his war time service; 67 photographs. --
   Provided by publisher
BIO026000   BIOGRAPHY & AUTOBIOGRAPHY/Personal Memoirs
BIO008000   BIOGRAPHY & AUTOBIOGRAPHY/Military
HIS027100   HISTORY/Military/World War II

TO
My Dad

We Interrupt This Broadcast ...

CONTENTS

We Interrupt This Broadcast ...

ACKNOWLEDGMENTS

I would like to acknowledge and thank the following for their help –

Father Van Rooy, O.P., M.A., one of my English teachers at Fenwick High School (class of 1941), a school where all the teachers were priests of the Order of St. Dominic. He had the remarkable ability to make his English class enjoyable besides informative. It was one of the most popular of all our classes.

Artist Angela Serre, for her for her artistry in designing and creating my book cover.

My daughter Kathleen Schutte and sons Robert and Paul for their persistence in urging me to put this little book together. It never would have happened without them.

My son-in-law Paul Cameron Schutte, our family computer guru, for his computer work preparing photos for publication in the book.

Mrs. Karen Stone, of Waldenhouse Publishers, for her patience and help in guiding me through all the many complexities involved in publishing a book.

We Interrupt This Broadcast ...

INTRODUCTION

I am aware the English speaking world is not waiting with bated breath for another WW II book, especially a WW II book with no shooting or heroics. On my final day on the firing line in basic training, I fired my last clip of live ammo. I never fired another round in the war, so let the reader be warned.

However, I am prompted to write anyway, after seventy five years, because my family has been pressing me to write of my experience, and because of a talk given to us by a lieutenant colonel on the first morning of our basic training at Camp Kohler, an army Signal Corps camp about twenty miles north of Sacramento. He was a crusty old bird and said he wanted to make something very clear.

He said, "While it's unlikely many of us will be on the front lines facing the enemy, we are in a large and vital part of the army and the war – we are a support group – and giving support and comfort to the combat troops on the front lines and also other non-combat troops everywhere is our primary mission. Fighting a war on two fronts thousands of miles away means they needed the very best medical attention, the best possible food, clothing, cutting edge weaponry and intelligence if they are going to prevail. And this is where we come in.

"They need state of the art communication with each other and with the command posts in the rear, and it's up to us to see they get it. And, very important, we need to see that all troops get mail from home as quickly as possible."

He said, after being overseas for many months, it's a tremendous morale boost to get a warm and friendly letter from home – a reminder of why we are fighting.

He said he hoped this talk would help us understand how vital our mission was to winning the war. With that he wished us Godspeed and good luck, and we began the task of being converted from civilian to soldier in the United States Army.

I have never forgotten that little talk. And so, writing this especially for my family, bland as it may be, typos and all, here is my little WW II story...

PROLOGUE

It is important to understand America's attitude and concept of foreign countries during the 1930's. It was much different from today. Today the world is so small London and Paris are 6 or 7 hours or less from New York or Boston, but in the 30's there was no transcontinental flying. London and Paris were five to eight days away. There were a few flights by flying boats in the late 30's, but as soon as the war started, any long distance planes were commandeered by the military. Overseas passenger service didn't start until after the war.

During those days we were aware of the struggles in Europe and Asia, but it seemed far away, and here a group known as Isolationists were very powerful, arguing that we were protected and insulated by two enormous bodies of water. We were coming out of the depression, and we should let Europe and Asia fight their own battles.

Hitler's anti-Semitic ranting did not cause a big stir. Sadly, there was a much greater tolerance of anti-Semitism in the country than today. I didn't hear it at home or at school, but I heard it on the street. There was a sizeable German-American movement here called the German-American Bund. They held rallies and parades, carried the Nazi flag alongside the Stars and Stripes and gave anti-Semitic speeches patterned after Hitler's hate speeches.

New York 1949. The Hitler salute with the American flag, Nazi flag, and portrait of George Washington in the background.

After Pearl Harbor the Bund and Isolationists dissolved almost overnight.

Prior to December 7, Congress and Roosevelt were concerned with what was happening in Asia and Europe. Congress passed the Selective Training and Service act in September of 1940. By 1941 all men between 18 and 45 had to register. The call to join the service was a letter starting with "Greetings," and it gave a date to report to the draft board for an interview and a physical.

The names were selected on a lottery system; it could be six months or two or more years before you were called, and then you were given 60 days to get your affairs in order. During the 60 day period you had the option of enlisting, and enlisting had its advantages and disadvantages. You could request which service you wanted – marines, navy, army or merchant marine, and the fact you enlisted was marked on your dog tags, but you were committed to three years. If you were drafted you entered the army and served wherever the army chose with no limit on time.

I registered for the draft and waited for my call.

Paul Sikorski

- 1 -

WE INTERRUPT THIS BROADCAST ...

The Chicago Cardinals (currently the Arizona Cardinals) were trailing the Bears by two touchdowns. They were playing at the Cardinals' home field, Comiskey Park, home of the Chicago White Sox. The Bears played at Wrigley Field, home of the Chicago Cubs. It was a chilly but clear Sunday afternoon. I was resting comfortably in my father's easy chair listening to the game. It was Sunday, December 7, 1941. I had graduated from high school just six months earlier.

The sports announcer describing the game suddenly paused and there was silence, probably for twenty or thirty seconds. Then a different voice came on to say, "We interrupt this broadcast for a special announcement: Japan has bombed Pearl

Harbor in Honolulu. We will bring you more information as we receive it."

My initial reaction was two-fold: why would Japan drop bombs on us, and was anyone hurt? The program switched back to the football game. The Bears won, 34 to 21.

I left the radio on, and shortly thereafter more news started coming in, and it was disturbing. Indeed there were casualties, and further announcements brought greater casualty numbers, including fatalities. The gravity increased with each news bulletin. The next morning the *Chicago Tribune* and *Herald Examiner* carried huge headlines. All radio programs continually gave updates. In those early hours the initial news was confined to casualties. The War Department restricted news of damage to keep the Japanese from assessing the success of the attack.

President Franklin Roosevelt addressed the nation later that day. Many felt it was his finest speech. He referred to December 7, 1941, as a date that will live in infamy. His final words were, "With confidence in our armed forces – with the unbounding determination of our people – we will gain the inevitable triumph – so help us God. I ask

that the Congress declare that since the un-
provoked and dastardly attack by Japan on
Sunday, December 7, 1941, a state of war
has existed between the United States and
the Japanese Empire." With little or no in-
dication it was imminent, the United States
was at war.

In his speech Roosevelt confirmed the
attack had caused severe damage to American army and naval forces, particularly the
navy, and many lives had been lost. News
reports in the days that followed were more
specific. The most appalling news was of the
USS Arizona. Over 1100 men and officers,
asleep in their berths, were sent to a horrific death as a bomb penetrated the ammo
magazine and exploded.

And just four days later, while the country was still stunned, another grim piece of
news was in the headlines. Hitler declared
war on the United States. It was terrible
news. We weren't prepared for war, but now
we were suddenly at war and on two fronts,
and Hitler and Japan had amassed the most
colossal military forces in world history.

So the remainder of the '41/'42 winter
was a time of very little good news. It seemed
all the news was bad. There was just one

good report, and it came out of Russia. Hitler, for the first time, had to retreat. He had invaded Russia in June of 1941, five months before Pearl Harbor. Hitler had prepared for the attack for more than a year. As part of his plan he offered to sign a non-aggression pact with Stalin, and Stalin foolishly agreed. Hitler's intelligence told him the Russian army was in disarray, with poor morale and old equipment.

It was quite true, and so Hitler's time table called for his blitzkrieg warfare to give him the keys to Moscow, followed by a Russian surrender in just six weeks, well before the Russian winter set in. He came close to accomplishing it.

By December the Germans were within sight of Moscow, but the Russians recovered from the onslaught, brought in many troops from outlying areas, and were able to hold off the Nazi armies until the cold weather set in. That year Russia had one of its fiercest winters, and the German troops weren't ready. They lacked winter clothing and their mechanical equipment – tanks and artillery – didn't have the proper lubricant to operate in below zero temperatures. Hitler retreated and fell back to reorganize for the spring.

It was good news, but had little impact on America's situation. The 1941/42 winter was a black winter in the United States, with rumors Japan was planning an invasion somewhere along the west coast.

Then something happened in April that changed the gloom to hope. An Army Air Corps Lt. Colonel named Jimmy Doolittle led 16 B-25 bombers on a bombing raid over Tokyo. The headlines were huge, "TOKYO BOMBED!" The raid wasn't intended to accomplish much militarily, but the morale boost was magical. It was a forerunner of what was to come.

But despite the bad news, America held three aces in its hand. First, while the army was woeful and the navy was crippled, America's manufacturing might was anything but woeful. Second, the country was outraged and unified as never before. Third, and most important of all, there was a massive pool of young men ready and eager to be turned into a fighting force and avenge Pearl Harbor and respond to Hitler's declaration of war.

We Interrupt This Broadcast ...

– 2 –

I JOIN THE LABOR FORCE

I did what many others did after I registered for the draft; I looked for a job in a defense plant. I wanted to buy a car and have some enjoyment before I was called. Getting a job was easy because there was a shortage of manpower, but the jobs were not substantial or with a future, because it was taken for granted you would be called. I had a bit of luck. A family friend was a union business agent for the machinists union and offered to get me a job in a defense plant. I wasn't sure what I was getting into but quickly agreed.

Two weeks later he gave me an address and told me to report for work. By then I had purchased a used car – a 1936 Ford, the last model Ford made with mechanical (cable) brakes. The purchase price was $165.00.

My first car, a 1939 Ford with cable brakes and a waterproof fabric roof.

The plant was the Goss Printing Press Company, a major company with three large buildings located west of downtown Chicago, about a thirty minute drive from my parents' house. It manufactured huge presses for printing newspaper.

My friend meant well. He explained that if I was interested, this job had a future. I would start out in a menial job, but he had requested I be considered for a machinist apprenticeship when it opened. He said a certified machinist was a skilled tradesman, earned good money and was always in demand, and a job would be waiting for me after the war. I had to join the machinists union. I don't remember the dues but they were minimal.

On the appointed day I parked in the employee parking lot of the Goss Printing Press Company, ready for a new venture, which turned out to be an adventure venture. I was ushered into the office of the Director of Personnel, a friendly fellow who told me I was going to be a timekeeper in the turret building across the street. But first I would go to the office and spend a day learning my timekeeper duties. I spent the rest of the day studying the forms to be filled out for each of the jobs.

They kept referring to turrets, and I wasn't sure what they meant. At the end of the day one of the office girls took me across the street and introduced me to my foreman, a big friendly man named George, who welcomed me. He showed me my desk, a high narrow metal desk with a stool. It was out on the floor of the shop next to his office. On the other side of George's office was the tool crib, with a manager who kept records on all tools issued for work.

The building was rectangular in shape, about 200 feet in length and 100 feet wide with a high ceiling of at least 100 feet. There was a track attached to the ceiling running the length of the building. This was the track for the turret lift mechanism. A lift operator would climb a narrow ladder and sit in a seat at the lift controls, wait for signals from the floor, and lift and move the turrets.

I discovered what the turrets were. We were doing the final finishing on pairs of turrets for five inch naval guns, and I was awed. The turrets came in from a foundry. They looked like giant wheels, about ten feet in diameter, and the work surface was a twelve inch wide surface, finished on one side, that ran around the outer edge, like a rim. They were positioned with the finished side up, ready to be worked on. Each weighed more than a ton.

While they appeared finished, the bearing surface was only milled flat, and that was where the machinist work was needed. The surface had to be absolutely flat. When finished, they were used in pairs. The bottom turret was fastened to the ship and roller bearings were positioned on the surface. The gun was attached to the top turret, and the gunnery officer would control its movement.

To make the surface perfectly flat, the lift operator would pick up a raw turret and lower it onto a work station. It would rest about two feet off the floor and the machinists, six to a turret, would seat themselves on low chairs or boxes at the edge. There were four work stations, four turrets.

When the raw turret was positioned, face up, the machinists would signal the lift operator and he would bring in a die turret. It appeared to be the same as all the others but was much different. It had come out of the tool and die shop and was flawlessly flat. The lift operator would pick it up and lower it to about five feet off the floor. The machinists would paint it with a blue liquid they called gentian blue. Then the operator would lower in it slowly on top of the milled surface, and the workers, grabbing spokes of the turret, would twist it about two feet clockwise and signal for the die to be removed.

Now the work surface of the raw piece was no longer silver; it was dappled blue and silver. All the blue spots were high spots and had to be scraped with hand scrapers. This took time. When they had removed the greater part of the blue spots, the surface was washed and the process repeated until the raw turret had a surface as blue as the die. About six hours was spent on each piece.

When it was finished, a government inspector was called. He would inspect the turret, sign the work ticket, and the turret would be washed for the last time and carried down to the end of the building to be prepped for shipment to a navy yard.

My job was to handle the paper work on each of the turrets, filling out forms, keeping track of the time spent on each one, and sending the paper work up to the main office. It took me about a week to settle into a rhythm and gain confidence in my task. After that, I had a pleasant surprise. I discovered I wasn't a young outsider working with strangers. The men knew I was waiting for my call, and I would be entering service sooner or later, and therefore I was readily accepted as one of the group. I was among friends.

There was no machinery operating in our building, so conversation was easy. In keeping tab on the turrets, I was free to grab a box and sit down and listen. It became clear I was back in school. I was attending a university with three majors: sports, war and sex.

Chicago had two major league baseball teams and two NFL football teams. I was a sports fan but wasn't able to keep up with the discussions of players and averages and win/loss standings etc., so I just listened and learned.

With the war, nearly every one of the men had a relative or friend who was in service, some overseas. All mail coming in from overseas was censored, but there was speculation and reading between the lines, plus discussion of the latest news on battle developments, etc.

Sex was the most educational. Discussions of the female torso and mating activities covered lessons in biology definitely not covered in any of my biology classes at Fenwick High School. There was no limit on what might be discussed, and it proved helpful later on in understanding some of the language the cadre used when I started basic training.

There was another learning experience not in my university curricula and that was tobacco. In those days nearly every man smoked, but there was no smoking anywhere in Goss. The men sought relief in alternates. Most popular was Red Man leaf tobacco. Next was Copenhagen snus, not to be confused with snuff.

Then there was an interesting incident that would occur two or three times each week. One of the girls from the office across the street would bring in or pick up some papers from George's office, and she had to walk almost the length of the building. The girls seemed well tutored. They walked looking straight ahead, no eye contact or smiles. The men behaved themselves, no whistles cat-calls or dog barks – total silence.

But all work stopped, and there was intense observation, then analysis and discussion after she was gone, mostly estimates on age and measurements. One of the young machinists who fancied himself a lover with irresistible powers of seduction would give her a rating from one to ten, ten being the girl of every man's dreams. In my time there we never did get a ten, but there were several eights and nines, which often led to a lively discussion because not everyone would agree with Lothario's ratings.

Then my big day arrived – it was Friday and the day I was waiting for. George called me in his office and told me there was an opening across the street in the machine shop. I was going to be upgraded to machinist apprentice! He told me I would need a micrometer and where to get it. This was big time. I couldn't wait to tell my father.

We Interrupt This Broadcast ...

– 3 –

MEET YOUR ENGINE LATHE

The machine shop was in a building across the street. I reported to the foreman and was struck by the atmosphere as compared to the turret building. It was much different. While the loudest noise in the turret building was the hum of the lift, the machine shop was very noisy; conversation had to be at a high volume.

And the air had a smell I later identified as a combination of oil and leather. The floor was wooden and black from lubricating oil. The high level of noise came from the power method used to run the lathes (a method now obsolete). The lathes did not have individual motors. Instead, there was one large motor in the center of each row of lathes, and there was an axle overhead running the width of the room. There was a large leather belt, maybe eight inches wide, running from the motor to the axle.

At the start of the shift the motor would be turned on and would spin the belt which would spin the axle overhead. Each of the lathes had a smaller belt running up to the axle and this was its power source. The machinist would engage his lathe and have power by lowering a handle on his lathe to engage his belt with the axle. All the lathes were in rows, ten or fifteen feet apart. Once the shift started the noise of the motors and the belts slapping made conversation difficult.

I was introduced to the lathe operator next to my lathe, an older and friendly machinist who introduced me to my lathe. The proper name is an engine lathe. My lathe was smaller than the others. He showed me how

A small engine lathe today. It has its own power source.

to operate the two wheels that controlled height and feed and let me spend a couple hours working them. Then he showed me how to shape my tool bit – a special hardened steel which had to be shaped a certain way, resembling the prow of a boat.

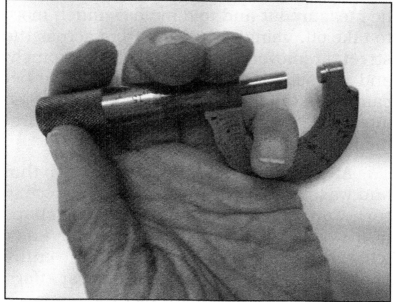

My micrometer. An engine lathe was useless without it.

The next day I was given my first job. I was given some steel bar stock about ¾ of an inch in diameter and a blueprint, and I had to shape the piece according to the dimensions on the print. It was fascinating. I spoiled my share of pieces and snapped my share of bits, but my mentor was patient and

I made progress. On every new job I would turn out one piece, measure it with my trusty micrometer and bring it to my mentor to measure.

At one point my lessons across the street were quite helpful. I handed him the piece, he measured it and told me how much more to take off, using vernacular from across the street. I removed another 5/1000 of an inch, and it was perfect. The approved piece became my standard, and all pieces of that job after that had to have the identical measurements.

After a few weeks I was in the rhythm and was turning out work. A typical piece to turn would be a piece resembling the shape of a wooden spool of thread. I never knew what the pieces were used for, but the entire floor was turning out work for the war effort. Each day was a new learning experience.

There was one experience I will always remember. During all the time there, on both sides of the street, whenever the conversation was on machinist work, I noticed any reference to a tool and die maker was treated with great respect. I learned that a T & D maker was a level well above a machinist, perhaps one level below God.

There was a T & D section in the shop, and on my break I would go over to watch them. There were six, all in a separate section. It was spotlessly clean. The men were better dressed, and their lathes looked new and each had its own power source.

I became friends with one, and one day while we were talking he reached in one of his shop drawers and took out two pieces of steel, about a quarter of an inch thick and four inches square. He rubbed them on his shirt and pressed the two together. He handed them to me and told me to separate them. I couldn't do it. I said they were obviously powerful magnets. He said neither piece was magnetized – they were Jo blocks. They had been milled and polished so perfectly (tool and die skill) that some sort of surface adhesion held them together, and the only way to separate them was to slide them apart. I was awed.

But Goss was just a microcosm of the total war effort. Henry Ford had retired, but Roosevelt asked him to use his skills to help. Henry bought the land and refused government funding to build a mammoth plant in a small town called Willow Run, near Detroit, to build B-24 Liberator bombers. At its peak,

The Ford Willow Run plant. At its peak, it turned out one B-24 Liberator bomber every hour, 24 hours a day.

Willow Run was turning out one bomber every hour, 24 hours a day.

I worked in the machine shop seven months. Then, arriving home one night and checking my mail, my "Greetings" letter had arrived. Uncle Sam was calling, and I was heading for military service. I had made up my mind on what I wanted to do. I was going to enlist in the army and request assignment to the Signal Corps because of my interest and work in photography.

I worked one more week and gave Goss two weeks notice. On my last day I thanked and said goodbye to my mentor and my foreman, and then I went across the street to say goodbye to George and all the turret gang, my original old friends. It turned out to be an emotional event I hadn't planned on. After saying goodbye to George I started the long walk out to the entrance and all work stopped. The entire crew stood up and applauded, and there were shouts of "give 'em hell, Ski." I choked up and waved goodbye.

Looking back, I feel lucky to have had the experience, especially with my turret gang. It's true they were a rough lot, sometimes a bit crude. I don't think I ever heard the word Nazi or Jap when it wasn't preceded by the F word. And often the F word was preceded by goddam. But there was no mistaking their patriotism.

When they finished a turret and stood back to watch it being picked up for the last time to be taken to the end section to be prepped for shipment to a naval shipyard, I could see the pride in their faces. They had fashioned something with their own hands that would have a direct impact on winning the war.

I am proud to say I was one of them, even for a short while. And when you add to them the hundreds of thousands of beautiful Rosie the Riveters, every one a true patriot and American heroine, the sum total was a labor force so fearsome Hitler could never match it. We never could have won the war without them.

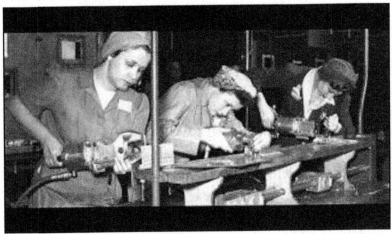

Three Rosies doing their jobs.

Of all the WWII posters, this was one of the most popular. It was never intended to be a portrait of Rosie, but everyone assumed it was.

– 4 –

THE ERC

As I mentioned, if you enlisted you could request which military branch you would prefer (but there was no guarantee.) I enlisted and requested the Army Signal Corps because of my interest in photography. In addition, the Signal Corps offered a training program called the Enlisted Reserve Corps (ERC). You were sworn into the army but continued as a civilian to take training in radio repair. It was a nine month program and you were on *per diem.* We called it poor diem because the pay was so small. The program began with three months in Jamestown, Wisconsin, then Milwaukee, then Chicago.

The Corps would arrange for us to attend class in a local high school. Some of the classes were during the day, but many were evening classes because of a lack of space. The teachers were skilled. They were civilians who had spent a career in communica-

Resistors, capacitors, condensers and vacuum tubes, plus the Morse code.

tion and radio technology. There were fourteen in our group. Classes would last four hours.

All work, of course, was with vacuum tubes. Transistors weren't developed until after the war. So we were in a field of resisters and capacitors and condensers and vacuum tubes, tech items obsolete today. We also had to learn the Morse code and the semaphore system. That was difficult, but for some reason I became quite proficient.

In Chicago we studied at the de Forest Electronic School, founded by Lee de Forest, commonly called the Father of Radio. He invented the triode vacuum tube and made many contributions to the science of communication. It was at this location that we saw a working television in operation, long before the post war television era. The school was on the eighth floor of a building in downtown Chicago near Lake Michigan, with a clear view of the lake. The television camera was pointed down at the Outer Drive, a drive running along the edge of the lake. On a cathode ray tube about eight inches in diameter we watched cars moving along the drive. We were in awe.

While my knowledge of radio construction and repair became useless after the

CONTENTS OF COURSE
TOTAL OF 572 HOURS

MATHEMATICS
191 HOURS

College algebra
Trigonometry
Introduction to Vectors
Analytical Geometry
Calculus

RADIO THEORY AND ELECTRONICS
191 HOURS

TRF Receivers
Super-heterodyne Receivers
Amplifiers
Transmitters
Modulators
Power Supplies

PRACTICAL RADIO—LABORATORY
191 HOURS

Detector Systems
TRF Receivers
Batteries
Power Supplies
Super-heterodyne Receivers
Analysis of A.C. and D.C. Circuits
Audio Amplifiers (class A, B, & C.)
Oscillators
Transmitters
Modulators
Use of Modern Test Equipment and Circuit Analyzers

Subjects covered in the ERC training course.

transistor was developed, I remained skilled in one endeavor, and that is soldering. We had it drilled into us – the importance of a clean surface on the iron, using flux, and where to apply the heat of the iron. I haven't used my skill recently but did use it quite often in my earlier post war days.

At the end of our nine months, I received a diploma certifying my completion plus orders to report in 60 days to a desk in Union Station in Chicago to board a train to Fort Sheridan for induction into the army.

– 5 –

BASIC TRAINING

I spent my sixty days with family and my future wife, Mary, and my closest friend, Burt Aamodt, who was accepted in naval officer school and waiting for the call. On the appointed day I took the local train to Union Station, was given my papers and boarded a train to Fort Sheridan with four others. It was about a thirty minute ride, and then we were trucked to the fort.

I was assigned to my barracks and my cot, then stood in line for a haircut that took some thirty seconds. Then on to the Quartermaster building with tables and non-coms waiting. We were given a duffel bag, and at each table we told them our size, and they slapped clothing and blankets on the table to be stuffed in the bag. The only surprise was the pair of shoes. They were heavy and laced to above the ankles. The most important item was our fatigues. We lived in those.

The next two days consisted of speeches, lectures and films. Three chaplains, Catholic, Jewish and Protestant spoke about the temptations we might encounter and how to behave. There were lectures on discipline and the importance of saluting officers. There were two films on VD. They were graphic and unsettling.

At the end of the second day we were told to be packed and ready to move out at 1000 hours the next day. We were heading to a Signal Corps camp, Camp Kohler, north of Sacramento. The news was not well received. Here we were separated from our families, not sure of what we were getting into, and now we would be moving three thousand miles from home.

The next morning we boarded a troop train. It was old, not very clean, and of course not air conditioned. There were three shelves built on each side with a thin mattress on each shelf. We moved out, heading west. Food was C rations and water. Breakfast the next morning was coffee and toast. It was a grim atmosphere, but then something wonderful happened. All rail transport was by steam locomotive, and steam locos need two fuels, coal and water. The train carries its own coal but stops for water. We were in

Nebraska and in the early afternoon started slowing to pull into a medium sized town for a water stop.

As the train came to a stop and we looked out, here were twenty or thirty ladies waiting for us. They were carrying trays and boxes. We opened the windows and they started handing us delicious sandwiches, home-made cookies and cake and cups of lemonade. There were well wishes and God Blesses. It was a tremendous morale boost; total strangers who cared about us. These ladies were angels. They could have been our own mothers. God bless 'em.

The next day those of us from the flatlands were amazed, winding our way through mountains. We arrived at Sacramento and were trucked to our barracks and cots. After the speech I mentioned earlier, basic training began. To a young man not long out of high school, basic training is a traumatic experience because the change in what you've been used to is so radical. One trauma is your first sight of a barracks latrine – a long building without booths or sections, just a row of ten or twelve commodes placed about three feet apart. And at the end of the row the last latrine always has the toilet seat painted bright red. This is reserved just for you if you have the clap. I never did see one used. And you no longer have anyone to consult with, such as your father or close friend. You see or experience situations that are unfair, and there is no redress. You do as you are told and don't complain, and there are three words that are absolute - "That's An Order." The Irving Berlin song about the army is a happy song, but reality can be unhappy.

The non-commissioned officers responsible for training you are called cadre. They are lifetime soldiers. Some are brighter than others, but every one of them knows the army from A to Z and is qualified to train. Reveille was 0630 (loudspeaker). You made your cot, had a quick face wash and shave and you were out in front of the barracks by 0700 for roll call.

Next was policing your area. Army camps are spotless because the "Joes" keep it clean. The platoon forms a front and walks forward in a designated area looking along the ground for the slightest bits of trash. The cadre loved to shout, "All I want to see are elbows and assholes."

After breakfast there may be lectures or films and there is usually a march of some kind nearly every day. Marching has to be in cadence, and sometimes there are marching songs or recitations.

After a few weeks we were issued our rifles. Ours were Enfields, made in England. We had to practice taking them apart and cleaning them. When we marched with them we had to hold them at the proper angle.

And there was the matter of nomenclature, something about which all cadre seemed to have intense feelings – such as what to call our rifles. Our barracks sergeant was no exception. He emphasized that a rifle is a rifle and not a gun, and never wanted to hear us call it a gun. Of course some would forget. When it happened there would be a small explosion. The sarge would walk up to the poor Joe, lean over red faced with anger and shout in his face, "Call it a rifle; call it a weapon; call it a piece, but ***goddammit don't call it a gun!***"

It was an important part of our learning experience. And I remember one thing about marching I thought was unique but made sense. When troops march across a bridge they never do it in cadence because it puts too much stress on the bridge. As you approach, the sergeant calls "Break step, march," and you deliberately break the cadence.

There were bivouacs, out in the open away from camp and we didn't like them. Each recruit is issued a shelter-half as standard equipment to make a pup tent. It is half a tent and at night you have to find a buddy to connect to your half and make a tent. The tent is about seven feet long, five or six feet wide and four feet high and you sleep head to toe reversed. It's tricky to join the halves and set the tent pegs, especially if it's after dark.

There was another training item we hated – the poison gas exercise. The horrors of poison gas in WWI called for being prepared if it was used in this war. The idea was to have us recognize the gas as soon as it was sensed. We were given gas masks and had to enter a room with a diluted atmosphere of a particular gas to recognize. There were four or five gasses. I remember mustard gas and tear gas. We entered the room with masks on, an officer (with mask on) ordered us to remove the masks for two or three minutes, enough to smell the gas. We learned there is more harm than just breathing it. It can also cause irritation of the skin.

Another item was both foolish and harmless, though the non-coms made a big thing of it. We had to crawl through twenty yards of mud, under barbed wire, with a sergeant firing live rounds of a mounted machine gun overhead. Of course we kept our heads down, and the worst part was having to launder our fatigues afterword.

Then about half way through basic there was an incident that I think is interesting enough to mention. Gambling in an army barracks is as common as inspections. Many do not gamble, but there is always a group which would just as soon gamble as eat. Craps and poker are the most popular, but there is one other type of gambling which was popular with nearly everyone – matching quarters.

It was popular because no one lost a great deal of money, but winning a few quarters meant much more back then because every camp had a PX (post exchange) and PX prices were very attractive. If you were a smoker and you won four quarters, it was all you needed to buy a carton of 20 packs of cigarettes. And everyone carried a few quarters to bounce one on his cot after he made it to make sure it passed daily inspection. If the inspecting officer didn't think your blanket looked as tight as a drum he would drop a quarter on it and look for a good bounce. If it didn't bounce, he would point it out to the barracks sergeant, and you would catch hell or worse, such as three days on K.P. (kitchen police).

Playing the game was simple. You challenged your opponent by declaring you could match him. You both took a quarter and flipped it into the air and caught it in the palm of your right hand. Then you slapped your palm on the top of your left hand and held it next to your opponent's left hand. If both coins were the same you reached over and picked up his quarter. If they weren't the same, he would pick up your quarter.

Our barracks sergeant was typical army cadre and we got along. He was short tempered but fair. He had his own small room at the entrance. It had a cot and a table and chair and room for his foot locker. Half way through basic training he knew our names. After our noon meal we usually had 30 or 40 minutes to relax in the barracks.

He was in his room one day and as I walked past he called my name. I went in, and he was sitting at his table with paper and pencil, apparently writing a short letter. He asked me if appreciate had one or two p's. I told him, and he wrote it down, then explained what he was doing. He was from the South and had kept in touch with some of his old friends. His preacher had just sent him a note with a ten dollar bill, a very generous gift, and he was writing a thank you note. He showed me the note and asked if it looked all right.

It was poorly written. I turned the paper over and wrote a brief note, thanking the preacher for a generous gift and explaining he was busy training recruits and asked the preacher to say hello to all his friends back in church, and handed it to him. He read the note, looked pleased and thanked me.

The next day one of the men said the sergeant wanted to see me. He was in his room. I walked in and he told me to shut the door. He said I had done him a nice favor, and now he would do me a favor, but I had to agree that this would stay with just the two of us.

I was intrigued, and agreed, and he told me to take out a quarter and match him. We both flipped, and I didn't match him. But instead of taking my quarter he told me to flip again, and again I lost. We flipped five more times and I lost every time! Something was wrong. You can't possible lose seven consecutive flips. It would be like getting a royal flush in poker.

He said he had seen me matching and was going to show me what to watch for to make sure my match mate was honest. He asked me whether I would like a head or a tail. I said tail. He tossed, and showed me a tail. He tossed again and showed me a tail again.

Then, slowly, he showed me what he did. He would spin the coin high, then instead of catching it in his outstretched palm, he caught it in his outstretched fingers. Using his thumb and little finger, he could turn the coin if necessary while he was transferring it over to slap it on his left hand. He explained he would toss his coin a tiny bit later than I did, and he would toss it higher than me. Thus when I slapped my coin on the top of my left hand, my coin would be exposed just a tiny bit before his, giving him an instant to look at my coin. In that bit of time he would catch his coin and, giving it a quick glance as it hit his fingers, would turn it or not, then slap it on his left hand, to win the toss.

To a match mate not watching closely, it was foolproof, because even if the mate noticed the sarge was glancing at the mate's coin, the sarge had already tossed his coin. It was up in the air spinning, so there was no way he could change anything, or so it appeared.

Then he cautioned me and emphasized not to try it myself. He said he was showing it to me not to make money but to know what to watch for anytime I was matching. If I spotted it, the best thing to do was keep my mouth shut and quietly back out of the game. I watched carefully in any future matching. It was an interesting little addendum to my army basic training, and thanks to old sarge, when matching coins ever after that, I knew when to hold 'em and when to fold 'em.

As the weeks went by and we felt we were learning, the one thing we looked forward to was getting out on the firing line, with live ammo, shooting at targets. We rehearsed our shooting positions outside our barracks and listened to the standard firing line commands. We sat on the ground with legs pulled back aiming our weapons. That was exciting, and the day finally arrived. We marched out to the range and took our places along the firing line.

I don't remember the distance from the targets, maybe a hundred yards. The targets were about three feet in diameter and the operators were in deep trenches below the

Ready on the right. Ready on the left. Ready on the firing line. Fire at will.

targets, well out of harm's way. An officer handed me a clip of live rounds and watched me insert it, then went through the standard commands, ending with, "Fire at will."

I approached this with great confidence. What was the problem? You line up the blade sight in the V groove and pull the trigger. Nothing to it. I fired the first round, and it felt as if someone took a baseball bat and hit my shoulder as hard as they could. If anyone had mentioned recoil I don't remember it. I aimed carefully and fired again, and it was the same thing. I fired several rounds before finally hitting a bulls-eye, and it dawned on me what made it difficult. I knew what was coming and would brace myself at the moment I pulled the trigger, which spoiled my aim.

I never did miss the target, but if you did, a red flag was waived for all to see. The flag was called Maggie's drawers. The Joes that were hunters had no problem. We went out on the range three days in a row. I earned my marksmanship medal but had a sore shoulder for quite a while.

Finally graduation day arrived. It was quite a celebration, with officers from other locations in on the reviewing stand and a band from a camp nearby came in. One hundred and twenty five were in the class. We marched in review, listened to a few speeches wishing us well, and enjoyed hearing our commanding officer confirm that now we were soldiers in the United States Army.

But then something happened. Before being dismissed, a second lieutenant walked up to the mike with a sheet of paper, read four names and told those he named to go to the CQ office immediately. I was one of the four. I was terrified. There is safety in numbers, and I wanted to be with my gang. Rumor was we were heading to the Pacific theater.

At CQ a second lieutenant told me to sit down. He had my form 20 in his hands. He asked me if it was true I was captain of our camera club in high school. I said yes. He asked if I did my own developing and printing of photos. I said yes. (I had entered it on my form 20). He said I was to be packed and ready to move out at 0800 tomorrow. I was being transferred to Fort Myer in Washington, D.C. to join a microfilm group. I was stunned.

– 6 –

WASHINGTON, D.C.

Fort Myer is the closest army base to D.C. It was and probably still is the most upscale of the army bases. More generals were stationed there than at any other base. At one time George Patton was the base commander. The honor guard for the Tomb of The

Christmas at Ft. Myer, 1943.

The Pentagon, Washington, D.C. At that time it was the largest building in the country.

Unknown Soldier (as it was known then) is stationed here. One of my first good impressions was the quality of the barracks and the food. I was assigned to a barracks with other Signal Corps men and discovered about half were former employees of Eastman Kodak in Rochester, New York. They were a great bunch and we became good friends. With one or two exceptions, our officers were also top quality.

Our work was classroom work, studying a special microfilm system the army had adopted to get mail overseas more quickly and more efficiently. After a soldier has been away from home for a long time, a year or more, a letter from home is priceless, but the current system was wanting. There was no airmail. Delivery was by cargo ship, and a time of two to four weeks was normal. Also, the German sub fleet was still taking a toll, and sinking a cargo ship meant thousands of letters lost. But Britain and Eastman Kodak developed a new method, using microfilm, where mail was delivered in days rather than weeks, and letters were never lost. It was called V-mail, and the army decided to use it for our troops.

What was V-mail?

V-mail (V for victory) was a correspondence system where the message was written on a V-mail letter form 7 x 9 inches. The forms were free and used for mail going out and coming in, (but mail coming in was censored). After the message was written, the letter would photographed in reduced size on 16 mm film. Two letters would be the approximately the size of one postage stamp. The film would be developed in the darkroom and packed in a small canister. Upon arrival at their destination, the negatives would be blown up to 60% of their original size and printed on rolls of photo sensitive paper and cut into individual letters.

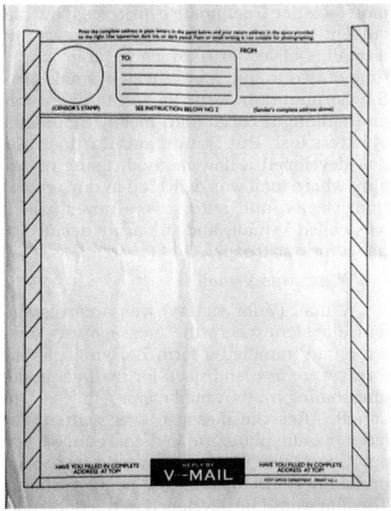

V-mail – First, blank form for writing a letter.

According to the National Postal Museum, V-mail insured that thousands of tons of shipping space could be reserved for war materials. The 37 bags required to carry

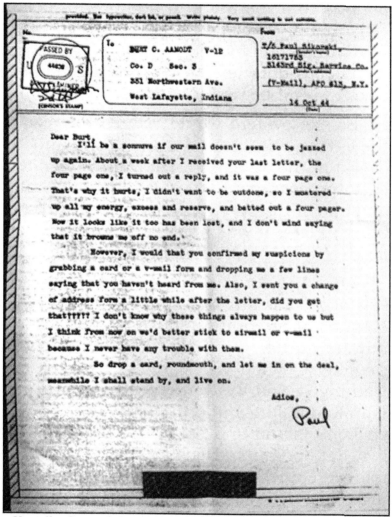

V-mail – Second, how a letter was delivered.

150,000 one page letters could be replaced by a single mail sack and be carried in aircraft. The weight of that same amount of mail was reduced dramatically, from 2,575 pounds to a mere 45. In addition to postal censorship, V-mail also deterred espionage communication by foiling the use of invisible ink, micro dots and microprinting, none of which would be reproduced in a photocopy.

So the system would reduce the size of the letter going out and then enlarge and deliver it at the other end. The darkroom needed to process the system (one in the States and one in Europe) was a large room, maybe 20 x 30 feet. It was noisy from all the water flowing and motors functioning.

After breakfast we would march to the Pentagon for our classes and processing equipment orientation. It was about a thirty minute march, past the Arlington National Cemetery. When we neared the end of our training period we were bussed to an Eastman Kodak film and print processing lab out on Long Island and spent two days observing that operation. Back at Ft. Myer we were told we could tell our family we were heading for a new assignment. Turned out the assignment was a transfer to Camp Myles Standish in Taunton, Massachusetts, the eastern processing camp where more than a million troops were processed, heading for Europe.

We were intrigued by one feature of the camp – the POW's – German and Italian, doing maintenance and landscaping work. We got very little briefing at the camp. Its main purpose was prepping us for shipping out by hitting us with shots, lots of shots. The system was a true army system. We would fall out and be marched to a medic building that was long and narrow. As we walked in the front end there were long tables with a medic positioned about every ten feet. We had to roll up our sleeves and go to each medic along the way for a shot.

I always remember exiting the building, because a corporal was standing there holding a hose with water flowing from it. I was curious and stopped to watch. A few minutes later I understood why. Out walked an especially large Joe. He took a few steps, looked up at the sky, then collapsed in a faint. The corporal walked over and turned the hose on the poor guy's face. He started choking and sputtering, slowly rolled over, got to his feet, and staggered off to his barrack. It was a typical army solution to a problem.

We were given two days notice to be ready to move out. We wrote letters and did laundry. When the day arrived we were trucked to

Boston harbor and boarded our troop ship, a former luxury liner, the SS George Washington. It no longer had any semblance of luxury. A more accurate description would be to compare it to a large can of sardines.

– 7 –

CROSSING THE POND

It was January, 1944. There were long lines of GI trucks at the harbor. After an hour or so it was our turn to unload and march up a ramp to the ship. Sailors were directing us and we kept going down to decks further and further into the bowels of

The SS George Washington.

the ship. Our area, same as the others, was an area full of hammocks, an upper and a lower. We stored our duffel bags underneath and were told to settle down and wait.

About five o'clock we were told to follow a sergeant to the mess hall for dinner. Before we left he told us we would get only two meals a day so we'd better clean our plates. The mess hall was a large area with many small standup tables big enough to accommodate four trays. All the evening meals on the trip were casserole style – a mixture sloshed out on our tray with two slices of bread and powdered milk or water to drink. It wasn't good, but we cleaned our plates.

Sleeping in a hammock is a challenge. I always slept on my side, but it doesn't work in a hammock. You sleep on your back. Later that night we heard the throb of the engines and could tell we were moving. No one got much sleep that night. The next morning we were told it was our turn for mess. The breakfast menu never changed on the entire trip – powdered eggs, toast and coffee or water.

Our own captain came by in the morning to give us instructions. The main instruction was to stay put, no wandering except to go to the latrine. He said once a day we would be allowed on the top deck for thirty minutes to get some fresh air. He said the trip would take twelve days because we would zig zag every seven minutes to make it difficult for submarines to launch a torpedo. He said we were in a convoy of troop ships, and it was the largest convoy so far to make the journey, and we were heading for Liverpool. There was reading material, and we were told to entertain ourselves as best we could. Dice and cards appeared shortly after.

My thirty minutes on deck was always late afternoon, before dusk. The air down below was stale, and on deck we took deep breaths of fresh air. We saw we were in a long convoy of ships. We got a surprise when we looked at what protection we were getting from the U. S. navy. I guess we expected battleships, but all we saw were a few destroyers, and they were WWI vintage because their smoke-stacks were vertical rather than slanted like the modern destroyers.

One afternoon was good for a laugh. I mentioned earlier as part of our training we had to learn Morse code and I did quite well. While relaxing one afternoon during my deck time the ship ahead of us started sending a message to our ship via blinker. I watched while it started blinking, "Now read this." I got excited and took out pencil and paper to write down the message to our ship. I knew I'd be a hero down below when I announced the secret message. But the full message was simply, "You may dump your garbage now." So much for military secrets.

On the sixth day out the latrine backed up. When we went into the john there was about half inch of liquid sloshing around on the floor and it wasn't Chanel #5. They fixed it the next day.

On the eighth day out the seas became rough and sea sickness set in. I was lucky; I've never had it. But it was obvious those who did were miserable. The procedure was to throw up in your helmet and empty it in the latrine. One of the gang got so sick he turned green, and they put him in sick bay. With two meals a day we were starving, and thought with so many getting sea sick and not eating we might get some extra rations at mealtime – a foolish thought.

The last fiasco occurred on the tenth day. An epidemic of crabs broke out. Crabs are pubic lice. They itch and they are contagious. The GI term for crabs is crotch bunnies, but it isn't funny if you get them. Fortunately I never got them, but everyone had to undergo a treatment, which was taking a shower. We were told to wear our helmets but nothing else.

We thought a shower was great because we hadn't had one since we left, but we were wrong. It was a salt water shower which meant getting the soap to lather is near impossible, and if you don't rinse the salt water it leaves a sticky feeling all over. It was quite a sight – everyone in the shower room was buck naked, but wearing his helmet. We were handed a bar of salt water soap and tried to make the best of it. When we were finished we held out our helmets and received one helmet full of fresh water to rinse. That water was like liquid gold, and a bunch of naked Joes going through all the contortions to rinse as thoroughly as possible with a little bit of water looked like we were doing some kind of ritual dance.

We reached Liverpool on the twelfth day, and it took most of the day to get us off the ship and dispatched. When our turn came to debark and board trucks, there were civilians lining the street welcoming us. I remember one old lady holding a rosary saying "Bless you, boys" as we passed. But we were in Liverpool and we made it here safely. We were told we were heading for London.

We Interrupt This Broadcast ...

– 8 –

WELCOME TO LONDON

It was dark when we arrived. We pulled up to an attractive three story house in a row of similar houses and were assigned to our rooms, four to a room. There were wooden bunk beds waiting, obviously built from wood used to pack supplies. We were given large sacks and told to go down to the basement. Down there was a room filled almost to the ceiling with straw. We were told to stuff the straw into the sacks, for our mattresses.

That night we slept in the deepest sleep we had enjoyed for the last twelve days. The next morning we were called out, had role call, then followed a sergeant to the mess hall, Knightsbridge Mess, about half a mile away for breakfast. Next we were told we would be allowed a bath. There were no showers in the billet, but the bathrooms and tubs were enormous. Then were told to wait for an indoctrination session. After a while we assembled to hear a talk from our captain. He had a prepared list of do's and don'ts and rules and regulations we were to follow as long as we were in these billets.

Everyone of course wanted a bath and we were assigned a schedule on when we could bathe. We were restricted to four inches of warm water, and told the King and Queen followed the same rule. Then we went to lunch, and after returning and getting a few more rules from our sergeant, we were told we had the rest of the day off and our duties would begin the next day.

Four of us joined together with one thing in mind – find a pub and try some English beer. We went out like babes in the woods looking for a pub and found one about a quarter mile away. We went in and it was deserted except for one little old man sitting at a small table. We had a discussion with the pub owner about which beer we should try, and finally got a pint apiece of mild and bitters. We heard British beer was warm, but it isn't. It is cellar temperature which is cool but not refrigerated. The barrels are down in a cool cellar and are pumped up by hand with the upright long handles at the bar.

We sat back and drank our beers, with much discussion on its merits. General conclusion was that it really wasn't bad. Then it happened.

The little old gent, who had been listening to us, got up from his table and hobbled over and said "Tell me, Yanks, why is British beer like love on the embankment?" We looked at each other, a little suspicious, but said we didn't know. He replied – "Because it's fuckin' near water" and hobbled off chuckling. It was our welcome to London, and we loved it.

On the third day we rode in a truck to our work station. It was about a forty five minute drive. The processing equipment for V-mail was in crates, and we spent a week or more assembling and running dry runs. Then the V-mail forms in mail sacks started coming in. It was steady work, two shifts.

To cut the finished rolls of photo paper, with hundreds of letters in each, we hired young ladies to do the cutting. They sat at small cutting tables. They would mount the rolls on the left, something like giant rolls of toilet tissue, and feed the paper with their left hand and operate a special paper cutter with their right hand. The individual letters would fall into a hamper to be sorted and forwarded. After a few days of learning it was amazing to see how fast they could work.

We were given three jeeps and started using these to go back and forth. Of course we had

Our home on Draycott Place, in Chelsea, London.

to learn to drive on the left but no one had any trouble.

We discovered our location was in an upscale section of London, an area called Chelsea. Our billet was on Draycott Place, near Sloane Square. There was, and still is, a fashionable department store called Peter Jones in the Square. We were in a private home leased by the army. We were packed in. Heat was available from a small fireplace in every room but the weather was warm and we didn't use them.

Draycott Place was a short walk to Sloane Square

The Luftwaffe was still raiding London but the raids weren't as frequent or as in-

tense as the Blitz of 1040. Now they only occurred at night when the cloud cover was
dense and consisted of approximately 100
bombers. In the blitz there were four or five
hundred bombers in each raid, and in one
period they came over day and night for 67
consecutive days and nights.

We lived here for six months. To walk to
our mess, Knightsbridge Mess, we had the
option of walking through Harrods, the largest and most famous department store in
the world. With so many men gone off to the
war, we were given a royal welcome in the
palatial Harrods barber shop and took full
advantage of it.

We had civilians living on both sides of
us, and they were very friendly. The owner
of one of the billets next to us was admiral
of the British Malta fleet. He wasn't there of
course, but his family was. Everyone knew
the Allies were going to invade the mainland,
but no one knew when or where. When our
neighbors would ask us when we thought we
were going abroad, we would remind them
we were already abroad.

We only had to wait four nights for our
first air raid, and it was a close call. A 500
pounder hit just six doors away from us.

We heard the warning sirens, but we were getting ready to go to bed, so we didn't pay much attention to them. But we knew when it hit. Our house was well built, but it shook the house.

We dressed and raced to the scene, ready to give any help we could, but it was a mistake. The air raid wardens started shouting at us to get out of the area. They had been coping with this since 1940 and knew exactly how to handle it and we were in the way. We stood back and watched. Ambulances and fire trucks and trucks with flood lights converged.

While we were standing there they brought out a gray haired lady on a stretcher. Her face was covered with blood, and we doubted she survived the night. It was our first introduction to warfare and was sobering. The raids began to taper off as the weather warmed up and the clouds weren't as dense.

The raids created quite a spectacle. They were always at night. The sirens would wail, giving about twelve minutes warning. Then you could hear the guns way off in the distance start up. You could follow them clearly because the noise would get louder and louder. Then the search lights would light up trying to probe through the clouds, and now and then you could see a glimpse of a bomber with the Luftwaffe insignia when there was a break in the clouds.

We were surprised at how low they flew and how clearly we could hear their engines. It was an unforgettable experience. The noise would keep getting louder and louder till the bombers were almost overhead, within range of the Hyde Park batteries, then all hell would break loose.

We were told this was the largest ack ack emplacement in the world, and when it

Hyde Park battery.

opened up you couldn't hear yourself talk. There were rows and rows of rocket guns and pom pom guns. There were portable guns mounted on vehicles that would tear around following the bombers, and sometimes it sounded as if they were just outside our window. After a while we could identify some of the guns. The bombers would drop flares which added to the melee, but none of the bombs from aircraft ever came as close as that fourth night.

And then there was an aftermath to the raids which I have never read or heard about, but which is a fact, because I saw it several times. It occurred when the chunks of steel flak fell back to earth and hit the pavement. When they hit, especially cobblestone, they would cause a noticeable spark. I'm sure it could be serious if any hit you directly. But it never lasted very long and most everyone would stand in a doorway when it started, similar to standing in a doorway waiting for rain to stop.

We were fascinated with London. It was large, and badly damaged by bombing raids but life went on. The underground in London is the deepest I've ever seen. It was running normally but didn't run in the late hours

Piccadilly Circus, the heart of London. The big Bovril display is touting a food item, a meat extract in paste form to spread on toast. It was introduced in 1870 and is still available. Now the display changes frequently, like Times Square.

The underground is so deep it assured total safety, and the trains stopped running in the evening.

because of the air raids. The subways had bunk beds and were a safe place to sleep.

The theaters around Piccadilly Circus were operating, but everything was blacked out at night. There were Red Cross facilities for us, offering food and drinks. There was a good deal of comradeship with British girls but very little with British soldiers. Their standard complaint was that we were over-paid, oversexed and over here.

To digress for a moment, my first choice today for a "must see" attraction in London would be the Winston Churchill Cabinet War Rooms, located beneath the Treasury Building in the Whitehall area of Westminster. It's where Winston directed Britain's war effort and is carefully preserved in the original condition of those times. There are recordings of his speeches, air raids, and photos. It isn't very ornate. His bedroom is particularly spartan.

But Churchill apparently kept his sense of humor. There is a small room along a hall with a plaque on the door which reads, "The Loo." But inside the room, instead of a commode, is a single telephone. It was his private line to President Roosevelt. In a quirky move to have something in common with Winnie, I have the same plaque mounted on the guest bathroom door of my townhouse. It's silly, but I've discovered when you become a nonagenarian people seem to expect a little silliness, so there it is.

There was one morning I remember quite vividly because several of us got quite a shock. One of the biggest worries always facing the Romeos in the group was getting the clap, the GI term for gonorrhea. Knowing when you have it occurs in the morning. Urination is suddenly difficult and painful.

One morning when a bunch of us were washing up and shaving one of the Joes standing at the urinal let go with a shout and an expletive, saying he had the clap. But then he went on to say,"....and I got it from Sister Theresa!"

There were gasps from all within earshot. What we didn't know was while the title Sister in our country refers to a nun, in England, at least at that time, the title referred to a nurse. He said Sister Theresa was a nurse from one of the local hospitals, so he got the clap from Nurse Theresa. I breathed a sigh of relief and blessed myself.

War activity in the sky was a common sight. Fighter planes were rare because their

Typical British resilience. A milkman delivering milk, walking through debris the morning after a raid.

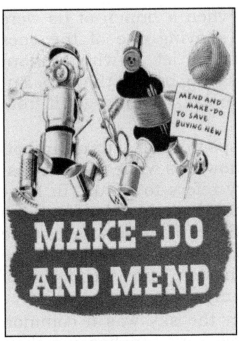

A typical war poster.

airports were on the east coast to conserve fuel flying into French or German territory. But bombers flew from airports in the west because they carried sufficient fuel to make the round trip. They would be at a high altitude and appeared to be moving slowly.

Our work at the V-mail processing station settled down to a steady pace. We became familiar with pubs and pub activity, the vast assortment of beers, playing darts, meeting Brits, etc. We were impressed by the fact that the British police – Bobbies – didn't carry weapons.

On weekends we would explore London. Hyde Park on Sunday was (and probably still is) known for free speech. Orators of all ideologies are allowed to climb on a soap box and shout their beliefs on just about anything, except they could not say anything detrimental about the King or Queen. The king was King George VI and the queen was Queen Elizabeth, known in later years as Queen Mum. They refused to leave London even during its worst months of bombings and were revered by everyone, including all of us.

Barrage balloons over London

About six weeks before D-Day I had an interesting experience, my first plane trip. The army had a system which allowed any G I to hitch a ride on a plane if there was room. You had to have a three day pass, and there was no choice of where you were going, so you ran the risk of not getting back in three days if the return flight was full. But it was an adventure, and three of us got a pass and got a lift out to the local airport.

The venerable C-47 (DC-3 in civilian life.) Far more books and articles have been written about this plane than any other. Some stories are almost unbelievable.

It should be noted this was the Army Air Corps, not the U. S. Air Force. All of the WWII land based flying was Army. The U.S. Air Force was created in September of 1947, two years after the war. There was a famous song at the time with lyrics, "Nothing can stop the Army Air Corps."

We were in luck; there were only two other GI's hitching a ride, and we were told to climb aboard. We asked where we were going. We were told Plymouth. The plane was a C-47, known in civilian life as a DC-3, The D stands for Douglas, the manufacturer. Many old air buffs will identify the C-47 as the most remarkable aircraft ever built. They are still flying commercially, as this is written. The airline employing them is in northern Canada, and in winter they remove the wheels and attaches skis.

Inside the plane there were only two seats – one for the pilot and one for the co-pilot. On both sides of the interior there was a long aluminum bench. We took off, and the three of us were like little kids. It was awesome. We flew over buildings gaining altitude, then a little later we were over neatly manicured farmlands.

We each had our own window and sat glued to them, pointing out things of interest. The weather was perfect, blue skies and sunshine. The trip took about an hour and a half. After about thirty or forty minutes it occurred to me that I was so excited I had failed to go to the bathroom since we left our billets. I had to find the head, and quite urgently. I looked around and didn't see anything that looked like what might be a bathroom. I went up to the flight deck and asked the co-pilot where the bathroom was.

He told me to go out the back door. At first I thought he was joking, but I was desperate and went to the back of the plane and opened the door. On the other side was a small room – it was in the tail of the plane so it was very narrow. I was confused at first until I spotted a tube coming up from the bottom of the plane to about waist high. For me it was truly a relief tube, and I made full use of it. In later years I would sometimes think of it when I walked into a washroom on a commercial plane. Obviously, this plane was gender restricted.

We landed at Plymouth, and the airport was close to town so we walked into town. We headed for the American Red Cross, our home away from home. We signed in to reserve our bunks for the night and then had a late lunch. After lunch we sat down with one of the local Red Cross volunteers and asked her to tell us a little about Plymouth. The young lady was knowledgeable and helpful.

She told us Plymouth's most famous native was Sir Francis Drake, the first Englishman to navigate the globe. Then there were the separatists who founded Plymouth, Massachusetts, and gave us the Thanksgiving holiday we Americans celebrate.

The next most famous resident was alive and well. That was Lady Astor, and we were given directions how to walk over to see where she lived. She said Lady Astor was born in Virginia, came over to Britain and met her husband, Waldorf Astor, whose

A popular pub in Westminster, packed with memorabilia of the world's most famous detective.

father built the Waldorf Astoria hotel in New York City. She captivated the social set with her irascible and saucy personality, then entered politics and was the first woman to sit in Westminster parliament. She represented the Plymouth area. Her career had many ups and downs. Her house was impressive, but not as impressive as the Red Cross volunteer's information about Plymouth.

We spent the next day exploring and visiting local pubs and talking with the town folk. The bomb damage was extensive, every bit as bad as London. We flew back the next morning, got back to our base on time, a brief but fun trip.

The D-Day invasion force.

On the morning of June 6 all the radio stations, ours and the English, were announcing the invasion had started. All activities including ours came to a halt, and we stayed close to our radios listening to news bulletins. About ten o'clock we got word that whole blood was needed and we were to head to our closest medic station. The common item for replacing blood loss back then was plasma, but now they wanted whole blood. Most everyone volunteered. We stood in line to give our pint, then came back to the billet to stay close to the radio.

The sky had bombers flying east in greater quantities than we had ever seen. The entire city seemed to come to a halt to wait for news. By the next morning it was a case of no bad news meant good news. The first wave was ashore and reserves were coming in behind them. The city slowly came back to normal, but with close attention to any news. We were all reading maps and learning names of small French towns as the Allies started to move east.

Besides listening to the Armed Forces Network and the London radio broadcasts, we could easily tune in news from Germany and much of it was in English. Of course the news was quite different. The invasion was a total failure. There was an Englishman named William Joyce who turned traitor and broadcast a Nazi version of the news.

He would tell us GI's how foolish we were being over here when our girl friends and wives were sleeping with 4F's back home. The Brits named him Lord Haw Haw. He continued to broadcast to the very end, then was captured and spent a year in British courts insisting on his right to free speech as a British citizen, but eventually he was hanged.

We Interrupt This Broadcast ...

– 9 –

THE BUZZ BOMBS

After D-Day England was alert to see if Hitler had any special response. Seven days later it arrived. A flying bomb struck London, in Hackney, and it was followed by many more. It was an ingenious device developed after

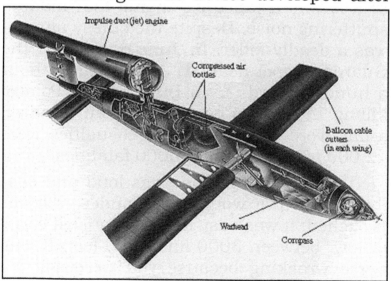

The V-1 rocket, or Buzz Bomb. It was Hitler's response to the D-Day invasion, and the first one struck London seven days after D-Day. Hundreds followed the first one.

years of trials. It was a small aircraft body, 22 feet long, carrying a powerful explosive. It was launched from sites in France and was programmed to drop on London. It was a terror weapon, because it wasn't accurate enough to hit a military target. It would simply drop somewhere in London and could hit a school or a hospital.

Hitler's plan was to spread such terror the Brits would demand Churchill ask for surrender terms. The proper name for the bomb was the V-1 rocket, but the Brits labeled it a buzz bomb, because its power source was a pulse jet engine that made a sputtering noise. Despite the cutesy name it was a deadly killer. In June one struck the Guards chapel near St. James Park (about a hundred yards from Buckingham Palace) killing 141. At its peak more than hundred a day were dropping. Total casualties were 22,000 with more than 6000 fatalities

The sputtering noise was loud and easily identified. It would grow louder as it approached. It was easy to see because it came in low, between 3000 and 4000 feet. It was nerve wracking because you were safe as long as you could hear the engine, but when the engine stopped you knew it was dropping.

I remember reading a London newspaper with a cartoon showing people walking around downtown, and each had one ear much larger than the other from listening for the bombs. The bombing continued day and night. At night the jet engines made an orange glow and could be seen from a distance of ten miles. We had access to the roof of our billet and at night would go up to watch them coming in. It was a foolish thing to do, but we were young and it was quite a show.

The Buzz Bomb caught the British off guard, and early efforts to stop the influx were ineffective. Barrage balloons didn't work, and being a jet it flew faster than aircraft. One method they tried with fighter planes was to fly higher than the bomb, and then dive to give them the additional speed to overtake it. I watched this happen one afternoon. We saw the bomb coming in, suddenly an RAF fighter plane, I'm told it was a Hawker, came down at high speed, leveled off and fired. There was a huge orange ball and falling debris. But this was risky. If the plane was too close to the bomb it too could be damaged or destroyed flying through the debris.

In mid July we were notified we were being transferred to another part of London, closer to our operation, a section of London called Hackney. It was more than a little surprise, it was traumatic. While Chelsea was upscale, Hackney was the reverse, almost a different world.

It was difficult to understand our neighbors. Not only did they speak with a unique accent, they had their own language. They substituted words different from what they meant, and if you didn't know those words you were lost. Some examples: instead of saying get up those stairs, they would say get up them apples and pears. Instead of saying "Can you believe it?" they would ask, "Can you Adam and Eve it?" Instead of, "Who's on the phone?" they would ask, "Who's on the dog and bone?" And I remember talking with a girl sixteen years old who had never seen Buckingham Palace, even though it was only about a thirty minute bus ride away.

Our billet had been a private home on Kenninghall Road, about six blocks from our lab, a small two story house, and it was very cramped. But we were only a few minutes from our operation so it was convenient. We were only there four weeks. The Buzz Bombs were coming over day and night, and one rainy Sunday afternoon we heard one getting closer and suddenly it stopped. We held our breath, and it dropped three houses away from us. We were told two elderly people in the house were killed.

It did more than break all our windows, it ruined our house. Everything was crooked. Some of the door frames were so out of shape the doors couldn't be closed. No one was hurt but three of us on the bomb side were temporarily deafened. The next morning we were told to be packed and ready to move. Trucks arrived and we were moved to a former police billet on Lea Bridge Road in the town of Walthamstow, about three miles from the lab. This was an upgrade. It was like being back in London. We all spoke the same language.

The V-1 bombing period ran from June through September or October, 1944, and what really brought it to an end was the advance of the Allied forces overtaking the launching sites in France. Paris was liberated in August. We were in London for most all of the Buzz Bomb campaign.

Then another secret weapon, the V-2 Rocket, started dropping about four weeks before we left for France. They too would land anywhere in London. This was a true rocket developed by a group of scientists at

Peenemunde, Germany, where Wernher Von Braun was working. It too caused casualties and damage before its sites were overtaken, but it didn't cause the anxiety Buzz Bombs did because there was no sound until it hit the ground.

Military historians tell us that approximately 2,200 Buzz Bombs dropped on London during the onslaught. We were here till the end of October. Not once did I hear a Brit even hint that Churchill should seek a peace agreement. The British were as unified as the Unites States. Then one morning we were told we were transferring to France and would set up our facility outside of Paris.

A V-1 Buzz Bomb is on display in the National Air and Space Museum in Washington, D.C.

Paul Sikorski

– 10 –

BIENVENUE EN FRANCE

We sailed from Southampton to Le Havre. On the sail they gave each of us a small GI manual containing translations of helpful phrases we would have a need for in France. Many just tossed theirs, but some of us were intrigued and had most of the booklet memorized by the time we reached shore.

In Southampton, boarding the ship to Le Havre.

We arrived late afternoon, loaded our duffels onto a truck and started a half mile march, mostly uphill. The weather was overcast. Our destination was a small field on the edge of a farmhouse. We were told we would bivouac here and to set up our tents. It started to rain. We hadn't touched our shelter halves since basic, so there was a good deal of confusion, arguing, and frustration.

In the middle of all this, eight of our comrades disappeared, then came back after a while to tell us how smart they were. We were close to a barn and they decided to explore. They discovered the barn had a hayloft loaded with warm dry hay. This was their bed for the night and after chow they

Heading for France.

bid us a cheerful good night and headed for the barn. The rain continued. We were exhausted and crawled into our tents for some welcome sleep.

About one o'clock in the morning we were awakened by a commotion. There was heated arguing and cursing and accusations. The eight hayloft dwellers had rejoined us and were trying to assemble their shelter halves in the pitch dark and the rain. It seems after they fell asleep in the warm dry hay they discovered they weren't the only ones enjoying the warm dry hay. They had to share their warm dry hay with rats - lots of rats - and the rats were running all over the eight intruders. The intruders were not happy and had to evacuate. They got zero sympathy from the rest of us and not much sleep.

Trucks arrived in the morning and we were told we were heading for Paris. That was exciting except a GI truck is not a good sight-seeing vehicle. The only thing you see is where you've been. We could tell when we were driving through Paris, but kept going until we were out in the country again.

We finally arrived at our destination and it was a pleasant surprise – an abandoned gated hospital complex: three cottages and

Entrance to our base in France. Tirpitz is the name of Admiral Von Tirpitz, founder of the modern German navy.

a seven story main building. It was located out in the country, northeast of Paris. The complex had been occupied by the German army, and obviously they departed in a hurry after a fight. There were shell marks on the outside of the main building and an abandoned Sherman tank in a field about a quarter mile away. The locals had cleaned out anything of value but there was plenty of evidence remaining.

We were assigned to the hospital rooms, two bunk beds per room. There was an armoire in each room. On the inside door of ours there was a photo of an attractive young lady in a bathing suit with the words "mein liebling" written underneath. There was a shower room on each floor, a welcome sight. Another welcome sight was a medium sized swimming pool on the grounds. It was empty. The officers lived in the cottages.

Photo tacked up on our armoire, dated July 1944. Paris was liberated in August.

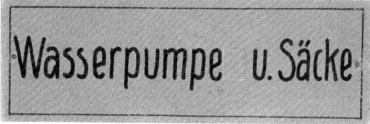

Also on our armoire.

The electricity was insufficient for our needs and a diesel generator arrived which some of our own men installed. Our processing equipment arrived from London and we assembled it, made dry runs, and the sacks of cassettes started arriving shortly after.

We checked maps to see where we were and discovered we were between two tiny towns, Villepinte and Sevran, and the closest city was Aulnay-sous-Bois. The towns were not impressive. The houses were very small and not all the streets were paved.

When we started our operation we hired local girls to operate the cutting devices, and we were besieged with girls wanting to work.

The Nazis lived well in France, but not the French. Here they went through our garbage every day.

View from our roof.

There were strong indications of the local residents being impoverished. When they learned we would put our garbage out each late afternoon, there would be ten or twelve locals waiting to look through it before it was hauled away.

We discovered we had easy access to the roof of our building, and it was the highest point around, so we had a clear view of the landscape, including Le Bourget airfield off to our left, the main airfield of Paris and the airfield where Lindbergh landed on his famous flight from New York. The closest city, Aulnay-sous-Bois, was about a thirty minute walk from our base, and trains from the

The children had no problem asking for chocolate. It's the same in French and English.

railroad station there would take about thirty minutes to arrive at Gare du Nord in the heart of Paris.

Our typical day was to get up in the morning, freshen up and go down to mess and then run the operation. Typical mess was oatmeal or powdered eggs. We hated powdered eggs. One breakfast treat was creamed chipped beef on toast (S.O.S.) A frequent desert was tapioca pudding, and the army term for that item was just as bad as S.O.S. Every Sunday morning we were served one fresh egg prepared as we wished. One fried egg is just a tease. So three of us who had bonded – Maynard Johnson from Lefors, Texas, Herb Simon from New York City and I agreed to give up our egg for two weeks so one of us could have three fresh eggs every three weeks. We worked a six day week.

Our bunks, made of packing crate wood. We gave up constantly refilling with straw and just slept on the wood.

Relaxing

Our main off-duty occupation was monitoring the progress of the war. The Allies were slowly working their way east and the news on the Armed Forces Network continued for the most part to be favorable. In contrast to London, we saw very little air activity. In time we had our system functioning just as efficiently as London.

Like any GI's in such situations, we looked for ways to make life easier without interfering with our mission. First thing we did after work was set up a rec room and a bar with a large sign – A U – Alcoholics Unanimous. We had access to local beer and chipped in to keep a good supply on hand, then hired a bartender. He was a genial old fellow whom we called Pop, and he was overjoyed to earn a few francs tending bar.

He couldn't speak a word of English but it didn't matter. It was here that I noticed

Alcoholics Unanimous, our rec room, and a few regulars including Pop, our bartender.

This was a field about a quarter mile away. Truly an example of coming in on a wing and a prayer.

In uniform, probably headed for Paris.

how strange it is for those who think if you
talk loudly to someone who doesn't speak
English, he or she will understand you. Our

My two buddies, Maynard Johnson from Lefors, Texas, and Herb Simon, from Long Island.

next move was to inspect and repair the controls to the swimming pool and fill it. That was almost but not quite as welcome as the bar.

The next move was exploring Aulnay-sous-Bois, especially on a Saturday night. It was about a thirty minute walk and was a medium sized city with all its amenities, including many cafes with friendly bars. Being in uniform was an entry anywhere. It wasn't London, but it was far more than Villepinte. The next discovery after that was the big one – Paris. With the operation running smoothly, we were eligible for a 24 or 48 hour passes.

I couldn't wait. With my first pass I hurried to Aulnay-sous-Bois and boarded a train and walked out of the Gare du Nord wide-eyed. I was struck by the beauty of the city. The streets were wide and tree lined, with attractive buildings. Parks and gardens were everywhere. Paris suffered no bomb damage.

The city was flourishing, but one thing we would have savored was not available – we were forbidden to go into a restaurant because food was still scarce. MP's (military police) were patrolling, and being in uniform we would have been easy to spot. But we had easy access to food at the Red Cross stations, and several had sleeping quarters available if you had a 48 hour pass.

There were no restrictions on French hotels. The Red Cross stations had good French wine and there was a French tradition we enjoyed. The tradition is that when the waiter brought you a new bottle he would leave the empty bottles on the table to show you were big spenders. The tables were very small, barely twelve inches in diameter. The challenge was to drink enough bottles so the waiter couldn't find room for the new one.

There was one sight that was not common, but it was extraordinary – automobiles powered by a wood fire. The combustion apparatus was built into the back of the car, the trunk lid removed. It would smoke quite a bit, but most noticeable was its slow speed. Other cars were constantly passing it, but it used no gasoline, and gasoline for civilians was in very short supply and expensive.

We were a long way from home.

The blackouts at night were strictly enforced, so crossing the street at night was as dangerous as London because automobile headlights were just small slits of light pointing down. Ladies of the night were prevalent, but they were not aggressive. They would offer a smile or a wink, but that was all. They had one variation that was popular because

The Gare in Aulnay-sous-Bois. Thirty minutes to the heart of Paris.

The Rue Royal, Paris. On the left is Maxim's and in the background is the church of the Medeleine.

it was harmless. A few GI's would rent a hotel room for an hour and a pair of them, with accoutrements, would strip and put on a performance they called 32 Positions of Love.

As time went by we learned more about what Paris offered when we had the time. We discovered we could stand in line in the morning at the famous perfume shops and they would sell a limited supply of their perfumes, in small bottles, at low cost. The most popular shop was Chanel, and the most popular aroma was Chanel #5. We shipped many bottles home. We discovered the cinemas carried all the famous Hollywood

Paris. Standing in line at the Chanel shop waiting to buy perfume to send home.

Notre Dame

movies of the time, but the audio was French. The Marx Brothers were popular.

Not everyone was interested in sightseeing, but a good many of us took advantage

The Eternal Flame, at the Arc de Triomphe.

of our days off and would dress up and head for Paris where, over time, we saw the Arc de Triomphe, Notre Dame, Invalides, Montmartre, the Opera, Tuileries Garden, the Louvre

The Olympia, the most famous music hall in Paris, located on the Boulevard des Capucines.

Doing as the French do, an aperitif and people watch.

Posing with a beautiful French mademoiselle and the beautiful Sacre Coeur basilica in the background.

and the Musee d'Orsay, Sacre Coeur, the Eiffel Tower, and the most beautiful of all avenues, the Champs Élysées. One thing very popular was to do as the Parisians do – sit at an outdoor café, sip an aperitif and people watch.

And then one warm night in the spring four of us had an adventure that made us the envy of the entire gang. Our first sergeant and two other non-coms and I were in Paris on a 48 hour. In the evening, after visiting several cafes, old sarge made a suggestion we couldn't believe. He suggested we try to see if we could make a short visit at the Sphinx Club, the most famous, the most luxurious and the most expensive brothel in Europe. Ernest Hemingway refers to it in his book titled *A Moveable Feast* about his early days in Paris.

We told Sarge they didn't accept enlisted men, and if they did we couldn't afford if we wanted to try it. He explained that all he wanted was just to see it in operation. It was just for a visit, and worth a try and it wasn't far away.

We told him he was crazy but agreed to give it a try. So we walked over and noticed we were in a very upscale neighborhood with huge attractive houses. Sarge rang the bell.

The famous Moulin Rouge. It opened in 1889, the same year the Eiffel Tower opened. It introduced the Can-Can and is still sold out night after night.

It was a large impressive two story house. The Madame opened the door, took one look at us, frowned and said, "The club is for officers only," and she said it in perfect English.

Our sarge, a former car salesman, was a silver tongued smooth talker and made a little speech, explaining we didn't want to patronize, all we wanted was to make a brief visit so that someday after the war we could tell our grandchildren that we were in the most famous "maison de tolérance" (as the French called them) in the world. He said we would talk to no one, just wanted a few minutes to say we were there.

She surprised us. She smiled, and said, "Five minutes", and motioned us to follow her. She led us into a large room that would have been the living room of the house and positioned us over in one corner. There was a beautiful well-stocked bar on one side. The decorations were luxurious but the atmosphere was different from what I expected.

I expected revelry, a lively, noisy ambiance but instead it was the opposite. Conversation was low key, with some soft laughter by the girls now and then. I only saw one civilian. All the rest were officers wearing the uniform of just about every one of the Allied forces. The girls, as expected, were extraordinarily beautiful. All were dressed the same, nothing but a long, sheer white gossamer gown and high heels. No one paid any attention to us and we stood there drop-jawed.

After about ten minutes Madame walked in and nodded. We gave our *mercis* and departed. I was quite pleased with myself because now I can say I have something in common with Ernest Hemingway. Both Ernie and I visited the world famous Sphinx club and both of us mentioned it in one of our books. In 1946 France outlawed all such maisons, so the Sphinx club is now just a blip in the history of Paris, but a happy memory for me.

And then one morning something else happened that was exciting, at least for me. Every two or three months a notice was posted on the QC bulletin board announcing promotions. It always created a buzz, looking to see who, if any, earned another stripe.

Our trusty Jeep was named "gig bait."

One of the Joes saw me at breakfast and suggested I look at the bulletin board. I hurried over and got a pleasant surprise. A promotion list had been posted. There were two promotions listed for master sergeant and one bore my name. I started out same as all the others, a buck private, and over time worked my way up.

Ten months previously I made staff sergeant, a nice rank, but master sergeant is the highest non-com rank in the army. He is the first man to approach the pay table each month. Not only is there a nice raise in pay, it's most always followed by a more challenging and interesting assignment. I now had a desk and an office. I ordered a supply of the new stripes and hired one of the older girls to do the sewing.

The U.S. Army newspaper was called *The Stars & Stripes*. It's foremost task was keeping us informed of progress in the various battlefronts, with maps and photos. But it also carried stories from home and cartoons. Nearly a dozen of cartoon characters were created in the war, but the most popular was created by a former infantryman named Bill Mauldin. He was a skilled artist and won a Pulitzer Prize for his work. He introduced

The Stars and Stripes

Willie and Joe, two infantrymen who depict-
ed the travails and weariness and danger
of the infantry soldier as it really was, living in the same clothes day after day, eating

"I need a couple guys what don't owe me no money for a little routine patrol."

Bill Mauldin cartoon. He understood the life of a foot soldier.

C rations and facing veteran professional soldiers.

General George S. Patton was offended by Willie and Joe; he claimed Mauldin was an "unpatriotic anarchist," and threatened to ban the *Stars and Stripes* from his 3rd army jurisdiction. He issued a decree that all his men stay cleanshaven. General Eisenhower told Patton to leave Mauldin alone.

At our base the bags of cassettes were coming in almost daily, and it was a busy time getting the letters out promptly. The girls working the cutting tables ranged in age from 16 to 20. They were a happy lot, sitting there cutting and chattering. After a while we knew most of them by name and they started learning a little English. This led to a humorous little incident described in the next chapter.

Addendum: A thought on the passage of time when I think of our visit to the Sphinx Club. The year was 1945. The publication date of this book is 2017. I would judge the average age of those breathtakingly beautiful young ladies in the club to be 26. So if any are alive today they are about 94 years old!

– 11 –

PARLEZ FRANCAIS?

I mentioned that when crossing the channel we were given a government manual translating English phrases to French, and I memorized the lot. Whenever I was working near the cutting table, I enjoyed trying to talk to the girls and practice my French. The girls welcomed a chance to learn a little English.

One day I overheard one of them use the term *anniversaire* – birthday. I asked about it and was told tomorrow was Giselle's birthday and they planned on singing happy birthday.

It gave me an idea. Why not give her a little birthday gift? I spoke with my buddy Maynard. He agreed, and we took a box and started hitting up the gang to drop something in the box for Giselle's birthday. We ended up with quite a collection of bars of soap from home, combs, scarves, cigarettes for Papa, tubes of toothpaste, packets of tissue, and a large assortment of candy bars. We wrapped the box in newspaper wrapping and I wrote "*Joyeux Anniversaire*" on the cover.

Next day Maynard and I gave her the box after the other girls sang their happy birthday song. (They use the same tune we do). She opened the box and was obviously delighted. It was a fun occasion, but we weren't ready for what happened next. The next day Giselle explained in French/English that her mother wanted Maynard and me to have lunch at their house next Sunday, to say thank you for such a nice gift.

This made us quite uneasy. Villepinte was not an upscale town, and these people were certainly not well-to-do. Eating food that was scarce was something we didn't want to do. But to refuse would be much worse, so we accepted and she gave us directions to her house.

At noon on Sunday, dressed in our uniforms, we walked to Villepinte and found Giselle's house. It was tiny, very tiny. Giselle introduced us to Madame and explained her father was off fishing with friends. It was a light lunch. We started with a lettuce salad and dressing, then we had sandwiches made with cold cuts and cheese slices on home baked bread.

It was all very tasty, but the tastiest of all was Giselle's father's homemade wine. It was delicious, and as Maynard and I finished our glass, Giselle would fill it again. The wine relaxed us and we sat back to enjoy the occasion, except that Maynard was one of those who had tossed his manual and couldn't speak a word of French, so I was in charge of conversation. But the wine helped quite a bit.

This continued until Papa's wine bottle was empty, and quite a bit of time had passed. I was not surprised, therefore, when Maynard leaned over, nudged me and whispered that he wanted me to ask where the bathroom was, and he added it was urgent. I wasn't surprised because I was feeling the same urge. I told him not to worry, I would handle it.

I turned to Giselle and quoted the exact words in the GI manual asking where is the bathroom. I said: "*Ou est le lavabo*?" Giselle smiled and said "*Oui*" and motioned us to follow her. We followed her into the kitchen. She walked up to the sink and turned on the water, then handed each of us a bar of soap.

I smiled, said *"Merci"*, and had no choice but to start washing my hands. Maynard did the same. Putting our hands in water of course made the urge more severe. So here we were, two idiots, washing our hands while we had to go so bad our teeth were floating. It was agony. We finished, and Giselle handed each of us a towel.

We dried our hands and I gave them my most enthusiastic *merci* and *au revoir*, and we hurried out. We hobbled, bent over, to the closest tree that was out of sight of Giselle's house, and let go. I knew what was coming.

Maynard said, "You and your goddam French." I knew he was unhappy with me so I tried a little humor. I asked Maynard if he thought now we should go back to Giselle's house and wash our hands after going to the bathroom out here. We both laughed except Maynard. So much for government manuals.

– 12 –

THE EIFFEL TOWER
STANDS FIRM

I was indirectly involved in one of the biggest and costliest battles on the European Western front, The Battle of the Bulge. The American troops were caught off guard and bore the brunt of a well planned attack. Casualty numbers on both sides were horrific. It was so named because a map of the battle lines showed an ominous bulge where the German troops had opened a major offensive and penetrated the Allies' lines.

Hitler desperately needed something to turn the tide of battle. He decided on a surprise attack in Belgium, making a straight line west to capture the busy port of Antwerp and isolate General Montgomery and his four armies in the north. His plan had merit – to convince Eisenhower to accept a German surrender, giving Hitler a chance to

Hitler standing on the balcony of the Palais de Chaillot, looking over the Seine to the Eiffel Tower. Of the millions of photographs of WWII, this was the most traumatic.

negotiate terms and free up his armies on the western front to turn east to cope with the Russians. The biggest obstacle on the way to Antwerp was the 101st Airborne, with headquarters in a small town in Belgium called Bastogne, but Hitler was confident he could prevail. After months of planning and preparation, he launched the attack on December 16, 1944.

Shortly after the attack started, Intelligence reported they had word that German soldiers who could speak English, dressed in American uniforms and driving American vehicles, were going to infiltrate Paris and blow up the Eiffel Tower. This was serious because the Eiffel Tower was then, and is now, an active antenna.

Eisenhower's headquarters, SHAEF (Supreme Headquarters Allied Expeditionary Force) were in Paris, and the Tower was his main communication source with General Montgomery. This affected all of us in the Paris area.

The M.P.'s set up road blocks at roads entering Paris. GI military vehicles were given special attention. Each was stopped and the driver asked where he was heading. If there was any suspicion, the driver would be asked what state was he from and what was its capital city, or something like, "Who did Joe DiMaggio play for?"

Our mess sergeant would ride into Paris every second or third day in a GI truck to pick up our food rations. He was born in Germany and came over when he was a teen and still spoke with a noticeable German accent. After discussion with our Captain it was decided he would likely run into delays, so he gave the job to one of his corporals.

Two days after the attack started, sixteen of us, all non-coms, were called to the Captain's office. He pledged us to secrecy and explained what Intelligence had learned. He said that being a communications situation it came under the purview of the Signal Corps. We were going out on special assignment to guard the Eiffel Tower, and we were told to be ready to leave in three hours. It was a shock, and we scrambled to pack our duffels.

Trucks were waiting and we were told we were heading for the dormitory of Sorbonne University. I found out later the Sorbonne is one of the oldest universities in the world. Marie Curie and Thomas Aquinas are among its famous alumni. At the Sorbonne we were housed in the dormitory. We had our own jeep and organized into four foursomes. One of the off-duty men would drive the on-duty foursome to the Tower and then take the off duty foursome back.

We were on guard in eight hour shifts and would rotate. We were four men per shift, one man on each leg of the Tower, and would change legs every hour. We knew exactly when to move to the next leg because church bells would ring on the hour. One of the legs was warm. It was a leg where we went down a few steps and into a warm enclosure underground where eight or ten French civilians were operating the radio controls, obviously working with SHAEF. Those two hours in the warm leg were our happy hours.

The worst shift of course, was midnight to 8:00 AM – freezing cold and windy. Paris was suffering through one of its coldest winters, and there was a blanket of four or five inches of snow. I was never so cold. I was reminded of what one of the cadre told us during basic training. He said when you are on sentry duty in the wee hours of a winter morning and about to freeze to death, you stay warm by doing what the famous kee kee bird does. You flap your arms vigorously around your body and cry, "Kee kee kee RIST it's cold!"

The obvious question – were there any attempts to destroy the Tower? The answer is no, but there were two incidents during the tours when I was on duty. I was the corporal of the guard. I was in charge of my tour. Both incidents occurred during the midnight to eight shift.

The snow was four or five inches deep, but there were drifts around the Tower legs of maybe two feet deep. One of my men on duty, Alvin James, barely made the height requirement to become a soldier. Of course we called him Lil' Alvin. He was on a leg diagonal to mine. All was quiet when I heard Lil' Alvin shout, "Corporal of the guard," the proper call when something isn't right.

I raced across to Lil' Alvin and got a terrible shock. He was down on the ground in a snow drift and thrashing about as if he'd been shot, but there had been no sounds of a shot. There was confusion and excitement until we got it straightened out. Seems Alvin heard a noise on the other side of the leg and went around to look. He didn't see anything but heard the noise again, so he gave the standard command, "Halt, who goes there?"

There was no answer, so Alvin released the safety on his carbine, at least he meant to. However, the way the carbine is designed, the button to unlock the safety is one button, but another button ejects the ammo clip so a new clip can be inserted. Alvin hit the wrong button and his clip fell into the snow. He was now unarmed, at the mercy of whatever made the noise. When I got there he was in panic, digging in the snow looking for the clip. He begged me not to tell anyone, and I didn't.

The second incident was something we discovered the second or third week after we started, and it always happened on the midnight shift. I was the first to see it and talked to the others about it. About three in the morning I noticed a little movement in the snow behind me. I looked closer, and it was a big fat rat, walking slowly toward the large wooden doors to that leg of the Tower. The doors were locked. I was curious.

The rat ignored me and walked within six feet of me up to the door and started gnawing on the bottom corner of one of the doors, trying to get in. He had already gnawed a surprisingly good portion of the corner, but still not quite enough to get through. He worked at it for about twenty five minutes and then ambled back to wherever he came from.

Obviously I could have shot it, but at that hour it was a diversion from the boredom. I mentioned it to the rest of the gang, and sure enough word came back that he appeared and did the same thing at about the same time every night. So we adopted him and called him Adolph. He never failed; he came around about the same time every night, did his thing, then turned around and went home.

Thirty years later, on my first return to Paris on a business trip, the first thing I did after checking into my hotel was to jump in a taxi and head straight to the Tower and to Adolph's leg. Did he ever get it the hole big enough to get in? Alas, there are no more wooden doors. Now they are heavy metal. I stood there for a minute, pensive, and hoping our Adolph died a more peaceful death than the other Adolph.

Our tour lasted four weeks. When it became obvious the Nazis were not a threat to the Tower, we returned to our base at Villepinte. Meanwhile, the weather continued to be overcast and foggy, and the news of the battle grew more ominous. The Germans had surrounded the 101st and the weather prevented air drops of food, ammo, and medical supplies, all of which were desperately

If our little Adolf ever made it into the Tower, he now has a fitting resting place.

needed. Each day a chaplain would come by and we would pray for clear weather.

It was during this time two things happened. First, the German general sent a note to General Anthony McAuliffe, the 101st Airborne commanding officer explaining the 101st was surrounded and demanding he surrender. McAuliffe looked at the note, wrote "Nuts" on it and sent it back.

Second, the 101st Airborne picked up a moniker they will hold dear forever – "The Battered Bastards of Bastogne." There is a very impressive commemorative monument and exhibit at Bastogne.

And then the day finally came. We awoke to sunshine, glorious sunshine. Our base was out in farmland and our main building was seven stories high, with a clear view of Le Bourget airport. We scrambled up to the roof to watch.

It was awesome. We never saw so many C-47's, one after another, taking off from Le Bourget heading northeast with medical supples, ordnance and food. They were obviously loaded, struggling to gain altitude. We reckoned they must have dropped everything to our troops but a grand piano. That was all that was needed. Hitler had failed. It was the turning point for the Allies' campaign on the western front, Hitler's last attack, and ended January 25, 1945. From then on Hitler was fighting a defensive war and three months later he committed suicide.

And so I can say with pride our mission was accomplished. With all humility I would point out the Eiffel Tower still stands firm today, in all its splendor, thanks to the diligence and endurance and devotion to duty of sixteen brave men of the United States Army Signal Corps.

We Interrupt This Broadcast ...

– 13 –

VE DAY

After guarding the Eiffel Tower, it was back to work. The cassettes were coming in every day and it was a busy time. But there was an aura of optimism. The Allies were into Germany in the west, and Russia in the east. We

Our office in the Base Post Office in the Gare Montparnasse. This was where Lt. Walter E. Stuebe joined us.

could see the end approaching and it was a good feeling. Discussions of post-war plans became more common.

But there was always one subject which caused a pause, and that was Japan. The situation over there wasn't nearly as positive as over here. We were still at war and still in the army, and it was possible a German surrender wouldn't necessarily mean a return home. But our war was over. Hitler committed suicide on April 30 and the surrender was signed on May 8, 1945.

That called for a celebration. We were confined to our base, but a notice went up on the bulletin board that twenty volunteers were needed for a special assignment. That was all it said. There is a hard rule in the army – never volunteer. But a few of us decided to take a chance. After all, the war was over. We signed up.

It turned out to be an incredibly wise decision and the envy of the entire base. The twenty volunteers were being sent to Paris to be part of a formal celebration at the Palais de Chaillot, a beautiful building across the Seine from the Eiffel Tower. Each of the various army branches was required to send a small group to represent their branch.

Paul Sikorski

We represented the Signal Corps and were ushered into the amphitheater. The curtain was raised, and here was the Glen Miller band ready to put on a performance! Of course it was sad that Glen wasn't leading the band. He was killed in a small plane that crashed in bad weather flying across the channel. He was flying to put on a Christmas performance for the troops in Paris. The performance at the Palais, including a couple speeches, lasted about two hours, and then we were free. There was no thought of going back to Villepinte.

The first thing we did was walk out on the main balcony of the Palais, facing the Seine and Eiffel tower. What made it special for the four of us was this was the exact spot where Hitler stood when he made his brief trip to Paris after the Nazis occupied the city. The famous photo of him standing there had a devastating effect on the free world, especially France.

And by now the celebration was in full force. It's hard to describe. I have never seen anything like it since. The city had gone mad. As we were standing on the balcony something caught my eye looking to the left. It was a twin engine RAF plane flying at just above the ground level. I couldn't believe it, but I saw it with my own eyes (and I was sober). It flew right through the legs of the Eiffel Tower and then zoomed upward!

There were four of us and we walked down to join the crowd. Men and women were hugging and squeezing and kissing and shouting. Being in uniform was a key to anywhere. We had trouble passing a café because we'd be invited in and handed a glass of wine. We headed for the Arc de Triomphe and then walked the length of the Champs Élysées to the Place Vendome.

It was pure delirium all the way. This continued on throughout the night. We bedded down at a Red Cross station and got up the next morning with serious hangovers, and headed for the Gare du Norde and a train to Aulnay-sous-Bois.

After all the celebrating, it was back to work, but much of the conversation was about home. The army had a monumental task on its hands. After bringing over countless troops over a period of years, we all wanted to go home at once, and that was impossible. In early summer (1945) a system was announced. Troops would be brought home on a point system, but we were still at war with Japan.

Combat troops, Air Corps, medical cases, and any others who may have served in harm's way got priority to sail home. This was not a surprise and there wasn't any complaining. Combat troops earned their priority. But it meant that rear echelon troops were in for a long wait and that included us.

On August 7, 1945, *The Stars & Stripes* carried headlines of a new bomb that had been dropped on a city in Japan called Hiroshima. Power of the bomb was described as colossal. Three days later another was dropped on a city called Nagasaki. On August 15 Japan surrendered. Thanks to President Truman's decision to drop the bombs, the number of American lives saved by scrubbing the need for an invasion is incalculable. Old Harry will always be my favorite Democrat.

The quantity of mail from home began to ebb. All censorship ceased. There just wasn't much to write about anymore and the number of cassettes coming in slowed down. Finally we were notified the V-mail system was being discontinued and would be replaced by the normal postal system. It took about two weeks to dismantle and pack the lab equipment, and we found out what our next assignment was. We were transferred to The

11TH BPO (Base Post Office). The location was the Gare Montparnasse, a railroad depot on the left bank of Paris.

The Gare Montparnasse had its moment of fame in WWII. In August of 1944, as the Allies were moving east and approaching Paris, Hitler, in a rage, ordered the military governor, General von Choltitz, to destroy Paris, just as he deliberately ordered the methodical destruction Warsaw. Choltitz agonized over the order and finally decided to defy Hitler. He surrendered and turned his garrison over to General LeClerc, and the surrender took place in the Gare Montparnasse. In 1965 a popular book, and in 1966 a popular film, was released entitled *Is Paris Burning?* quoting Hitler screaming at Choltitz. The German general was captured but no specific charges were ever filed against him. He was held in a military camp in Mississippi and released in 1947.

Here we became postal workers, sorting mail coming in and going out. Instead of sacks of cassettes there were mail sacks to handle. What was singular was the use being made of German POW's. They did all the maintenance, and those who could speak a little English helped sort mail. But instead of the vaunted SS or Wehrmacht troops, these prisoners looked like kindly old grandfathers. Near the end Hitler was so desperate he conscripted youngsters and oldsters to keep the war going. These men were happy it was over and were good workers.

Another morning we got another surprise. A new member was added to our staff, a former infantry first lieutenant who was seriously wounded but had recovered. His name was Walter E. Stuebe, and he was from Danville, Illinois. Walter turned out to be a sudden bright light in the outfit and especially in the office.

He had landed at France and fought his way east, leading his platoon through hedgerows and farmland. At one point, in a fierce battle, a German tank shell took off the top of his skull. A fraction of an inch more and it would have killed him. They flew him to a base hospital in England, and the surgeons fashioned a new skull made of silver. They grafted skin over it so that the scar really wasn't very noticeable.

After he recovered, the army told him he was heading home. He refused, and demanded he return to his outfit. They refused, but offered a compromise, a desk job behind the lines. He reluctantly agreed, and was assigned to our outfit.

Walter was a free spirit who changed the mood of the office. He would regale us with ribald recitations and songs. Somehow he acquired a U.S. Army Harley-Davidson and would race around Paris on it. There is no doubt Walter was one of those infantry officers for whom his men would walk through fire. He would occasionally talk of combat and one day told us something that is so far fetched it's hard to believe, but there is no doubt Walter was qualified to talk of it.

He said that after fighting through hedgerows it was mostly farmland, and as they advanced, they would sometimes come upon a farm that was still functioning. Sometimes the Germans would counterattack, beginning with an artillery barrage. When it started everyone would seek cover such as a ground depression or a shell crater.

The cows and horses and sheep and pigs would just stand there and be killed, but not the goats; they were smart. He claimed they knew enough to look for cover, and once in a while, when incoming began, you might dive into a shell hole only to find a goat was already there, and it was your companion until the shelling stopped. We loved Walter and felt privileged to have a true hero in our group. Of course Walter was one of the first to head home after the surrender. After the war I tried to contact him in Danville, but was not successful.

One thing we learned quickly was never complain to an Aussie or a Canadian about being away from home for so long. Those poor Joes started arriving in England not long after the war started, so they were there a year or two or three before we arrived, with no furloughs home.

But one aftermath of the war's end was the easy availability of furloughs, and four of us decided to see a bit more of Europe. Our furloughs were approved, and we made some plans travelling by rail. We entered Germany at Mulhouse, went on to Munich, then into Switzerland to the ski resort town of St. Moritz.

Switzerland was suffering from lack of tourists, and we were told we could enjoy re-sorts at rates much lower than normal. It was true. We had private rooms at the fa-mous Badrutt's Palace hotel for $35.00 a night. We signed up for skiing lessons but it turned out to be embarrassing. All the time we were trying to do as our instructor was telling us, little kids three or four years old were skiing around us as if they had been skiing for twenty years.

1945. Sketched by a street artist in Rome.

The Rome visit was great. There weren't nearly as many GI's in Rome as Paris, and we were welcome everywhere, including posh restaurants. We applied for an audience with the Pope. It was approved, and the next day we were in a room in the Vatican with about fifty others waiting for His Holiness, Pius XII. He arrived and spoke to us in Italian. There were about a dozen GI's and we were all together on one side. He looked at us, smiled and nodded.

The trip back to Paris was uneventful, and two weeks later our departure date was posted. We sailed from Le Havre, again on the USS George Washington, but this time we weren't nearly as cramped, and it only took five days. As we approached our dock in the New York harbor, we were all on deck waiting to see the Statue of Liberty. When it came into sight we were surprised at how small it appeared, but as we entered the harbor it was a beautiful sight and an emotional moment.

From New York we were sent to our discharge bases. Mine was Camp McCoy in Wisconsin. Then we were given an allowance for the train ticket home. At Chicago an excited mother, father, sister and future bride were waiting. My military tour of duty was over.

So there it is – a long answer in a small book to the question: "What did you do in the war, Grandpa (or great Grandpa)?" In looking back, I feel grateful and lucky, but surely not a hero. The heroes are those who didn't make it back or were seriously wounded. But all of us who served can share the pride in what we accomplished.

We weren't prepared, and we weren't soldiers, but we suddenly had to go to war on two fronts and face the two mightiest military forces in world history. But today, when our children file into their classrooms and stand up and pledge allegiance to a flag, it is still that beautiful American flag.

* * * *

EPILOGUE 1

The WWII Memorial in Washington, D.C. was opened with an elaborate ceremony on April 29, 2004. Washington was overrun with WWII veterans including my wife Mary and me. We checked into a Marriott two days early and joined the celebration. The camaraderie was universal. Meet a stranger, ask where he was from, what branch did he serve in, and where did he serve.

Bob Feller in his prime.

On the morning before the big day, Mary and I were seated at a small table and ordered breakfast. Another couple came in and sat across from us. The gentleman asked me where we were from. I said Chattanooga, Tennessee, and I asked where they were from. He said Gates Mills, Ohio, and then he said he had played baseball in Chattanooga, in Engel stadium. I asked him for whom he played, and he said the Cleveland Indians. I asked him if he ever met the great Hall of Famer Bob Feller.

He smiled and said, "I'm Bob Feller." That started a lively conversation because I had just sent a check to the baseball museum he founded back in his home town of Van Meter, Iowa. We met again in the dining room that evening and had dinner together.

Bob was a prodigy, the first pitcher to win 24 games before he was 21. He never played in the minors and struck out 15 batters in his first major league game. Joe DiMaggio said he didn't think there would ever be a pitcher who could throw as fast as Rapid Robert. Ted Williams said Feller was the fastest and best pitcher he ever saw during his career. Stan Musial said he believed he was probably the greatest pitcher of his era.

While at the top of his game, Feller enlisted in the navy two days after Pearl Harbor. He was a gunnery officer on the battleship Alabama, a ship which fought in both the North Atlantic and the Pacific. He spent four years in the navy and was decorated with six campaign ribbons and eight battle stars.

He returned home to the Indians and threw his second and third no-hitter, the latter with the Yankees and Joe DiMaggio. One can only imagine what his record would have been if he didn't sacrifice four years of his career to fight for his country. Feller played ball with Satchel Paige and was an outspoken advocate for bringing black players into the majors. He was a close friend of George and Laura Bush, and he and his wife Anne were having breakfast with them at the White House the next morning.

We came home and I called Mark Weidmer, sports editor of the *Chattanooga Times News-Free Press* and told him of my good luck. Mark wrote an article about two veterans meeting in Washington, D.C. at the WWII Memorial opening

Veteran Paul and veteran baseball legend.

ceremony. Bob passed away in December of 2010 at the age of 92.

Sports

Chattanooga Times Free Press   Wednesday, June 2, 2004

Veterans Sikorski, Feller meet

Two World War II veterans and their wives were eating at adjoining tables last Thursday morning at a Washington, D.C., hotel.

"Hi, we're Paul and Mary from Tennessee," said the first veteran.

"Hi, we're Bob and Anne from Ohio," replied the second.

In a few minutes they were trading business cards and discussing the weekend's dedication of the World War II Memorial when Ohio Bob asked Tennessee Paul what part of the Volunteer State he was from.

Mark Wiedmer
Commentary

When Paul answered, "Chattanooga," Bob informed him he once played a few exhibition baseball games at Engel Stadium.

Now was Tennessee Paul's turn to ask a question.

"So," he asked, "if you're from Ohio, did you ever see the great Bob Feller pitch for Cleveland?"

Ohio Bob chuckled for a moment, then smiled and said, "I'm Bob Feller."

"I could have fallen off my chair," Paul Sikorski said Tuesday. "I was having breakfast with a legend."

We will hopefully hear these stories for weeks and months, these grand moments from the greatest reunion of the Greatest Generation. Feller was already famous when World War II broke out at the dawn of the 1940s. Sikorski was living in Chicago, in love with his hometown White Sox.

The two never met during their war years, but that didn't matter over the weekend. They were simply two veterans, the 81-year-old Sikorski and 85-year-old Feller finally earning long-overdue recognition for saving a nation.

"I was delighted with the memorial itself," Sikorski said. "It's more beautiful than I can describe.

"But I was saddened that it took so long to build it, and so many who served in the war are already gone." The dedication was more emotional than I expected. Some men wept openly."

Feller could not be reached for this column. A personal friend of the first President Bush, he ate breakfast Monday with the current President Bush for the second time in two weeks and had not yet returned to his Ohio home.

But to understand what the Hall of Fame pitcher sacrificed to serve his country, the man won 24 games in 1939, 27 in 1940 and 25 in '41 before serving in the military. When he returned midway through the 1945 season, he won nine, then 26 in 1946 and 20 in '42.

One can only imagine how many games he might have won had he not become a gunnery serpeant on the USS Alabama.

"Everything was so different then," Sikorski said. "People forget that when Hitler invaded Poland in 1939, he had secretly amassed the largest army in the world. Japan was close behind. By contrast, we had the world's 17th largest military. To build an army like we did from kids on the blocks, kids with no previous military training, is amazing."

Sikorski served in the Signal Corps, making sure V-Mails arrived for the troops and that their responding V-Mails made their way quickly back to the States.

For those who have never heard of V-Mails, they were one-page letters photographed on 16-mm film, developed to two-thirds of their original 4X-by-11 sheet of paper and delivered from the U.S. to Europe and the Pacific in anywhere from five days to two weeks. Because of the war, there was no airmail and regular mail sometimes took as much as six weeks to be delivered to those on the front lines.

"I started out stationed in London," Sikorski said. "We handled the buzz bombs just fine."

But when the Germans began launching heavier artillery, the Signal Corps transferred to Aulnay Sous Vois, a village 20 miles north of Paris. From there Sikorski saw the cargo planes take off on their way to bring supplies to the weather-ravaged troops just before the Battle of the Bulge.

Yet for all the grim seriousness of World War II, he said American sports played an important role with the troops.

"You could say that it was a happy distraction," he said. "We all had our favorite teams — the White Sox for me — and we all kept up with them as best we could. We would watch for the results and kid each other."

When the war ended, Sikorski returned to Chicago about the same time Feller returned to Cleveland. Paul married Mary and started a family that would eventually grow to include four children, seven grandchildren and one great-great-grandchild.

Then a little more than 40 years ago, an old friend called offering him a job at Textile Rubber and Chemical Co. in Dalton, Ga. Four decades later, Sikorski says, "I want to work until the president of the company or God tells me to retire."

Feller is no less active, currently laying the groundwork for a Bob Feller Museum.

But if it has often been a happy ending to a lifetime well spent for those World War II vets still around, Sikorski also perfectly framed the importance of the sacrifice for both the living and dead of his generation.

"Our grandchildren walk to school every day under the American flag," he said. "It could well have been another flag, either the Nazi swastika or Japan's rising sun."

Amazing the legacy of one generation's kids on the blocks.

E-mail Mark Wiedmer at mwiedmer@timesfreepress.com

EPILOGUE 2

In 1965 when I was working in the U.S., Textile Rubber acquired what turned out to be our biggest customer at the time, The Ozite Corporation in Chicago, and it was my account. They had three large production plants, one in Milwaukee, one in Newark, New Jersey, and the third in Anaheim, California. I worked in rotation with all three and went out to the west coast two weeks out of every six. I would spend one week at Anaheim, then split the second week between San Francisco, Seattle and Vancouver working with carpet mill salesmen.

I was impressed with the Anaheim plant operation as compared to the other two. It was always spotlessly clean and ran smoothly. I mentioned this when talking to the plant manager and he explained why. His chief engineer was a former tank commander in Rommel's Afrika Corps in North Africa and ran the plant with German precision. His name was Heinz Kruger and he spoke with a heavy German accent.

I was intrigued, and we became good friends. He wasn't reluctant to discuss the war, and with my trips out west I would often make it a point to invite him to spend an evening with me. Over dinner we would talk about the war, usually with me asking questions.

One night I asked him if he ever had contact with General Erwin Rommel, commander of the Afrika Corps and arguably Hitler's best general. He said he saw him only once, in Africa. They were preparing to launch a counter-attack and word came through that Rommel would be arriving the next day to inspect the battalion.

By the next morning they had their tanks cleaned and lined up side by side. Each tank commander was standing at attention in front of his tank, ready for the big moment. Rommel rode by slowly in a staff car. When he came to Heinz's tank he told his driver to stop. Heinz explained that they would frequently "borrow" any items they came upon that would make life a little easier. He had borrowed a mattress and had it tied to the side of his tank.

Rommel frowned and said, "What the hell is that?"

Heinz said, "It's a mattress, sir."

Rommel was angry and said "Cut that goddamned thing down." Heinz cut the ropes and the mattress fell to the ground. This revealed something. The practice was for the tank commander to have an icon painted on the side of his tank for every one of the battles they were in, similar to the Americans painting icons on their planes for each of their missions. Heinz's tank had a long row of icons.

Rommel spent a minute studying them, then turned to Heinz and said, "Tie it back up," and he then told his driver to drive on.

I asked where he was transferred when they had to withdraw from Africa. He said Russia, and it was miserable. They didn't have winter clothing; there was no anti freeze for their tanks, and fuel and ammunition were scarce.

He said with no antifreeze they had a set procedure to follow each night. There was no tank warfare after dark, so all the tanks would line up side by side. The tanks were designed with a double port in the radiators. They would connect all the tank ports with short hoses, and run one tank all night to circulate hot water and prevent freezing.

He told of one minor incident which could have been a bad mistake. There was a lull in the fighting, and the Russians were on one side of a small mountain and the Germans on the other. A road ran the length of the valley between, and the Russians controlled it.

One morning Heinz saw a Russian courier on a motorcycle travelling along the road. He wondered if he could do it. He climbed in his tank, took careful aim and fired. He said he was spot on. There was an explosion and debris but no more courier or motorcycle. However, Heinz said if his commanding officer ever found out he wasted a precious tank shell on one lone Russian soldier, he would have been in serious trouble.

I asked how it ended. Was he captured? He said no. They made an orderly retreat back into Germany to the first town that had some transportation. He walked away from his tank, took a bus and then a train back to his home, and that was it.

And Heinz had a sense of humor. One night I asked him when and where in the war did it become obvious to him he was going to lose the war. He looked at me and said, "Lose, hell; we're gonna get you bastards yet."

Bookman Old Style and Belwe Bold MT on LSI 50# white
Type and Design by Karen Paul Stone

Master Sergeant Paul Sikorski, 1945

ABOUT THE AUTHOR

Paul Sikorski is a 94 year old veteran who spent his childhood in Riverside, a suburb of Chicago, attended Fenwick High School in Oak Park and is a graduate of Northwestern University. He currently lives in Chattanooga, Tennessee. His chief interests are his family, his friends, his church, and the well being of his country.

Paul Sikorski in 2017

CPSIA information can be obtained
at www.ICGtesting.com
Printed in the USA
LVOW03s0040130617
537896LV00001B/1/P